Best Career and Education Web Sites

A Quick Guide to Online Job Search

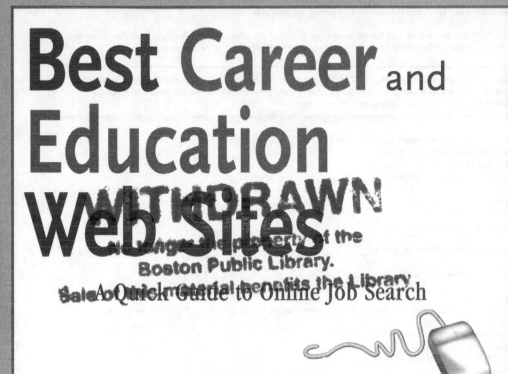

FIFTH EDITION

Anne Wolfinger

JIST
Works
America's Career Publisher

Best Career and Education Web Sites, Fifth Edition

© 2007 by JIST Publishing

Published by JIST Works, an imprint of JIST Publishing, Inc.

8902 Otis Avenue

Indianapolis, IN 46216-1033

Phone: 1-800-648-JIST Fax: 1-800-JIST-FAX   E-mail: info@jist.com

Visit our Web site at www.jist.com for information on JIST, free job search tips, book chapters, and ordering instructions for our many products! For free information on 14,000 job titles, visit www.careeroink.com.

> *Quantity discounts are available for JIST books. Have future editions of JIST books automatically delivered to you on publication through our convenient standing order program. Please call our Sales Department at 1-800-648-5478 for a free catalog and more information.*

Trade Product Line Manager: Lori Cates Hand
Development Editor: Gayle Johnson
Production Editor: Jill Mazurczyk
Interior Design: Debbie Berman
Cover Design: Nick Anderson
Page Layout: Aleata Howard
Proofreader: Linda Seifert
Indexer: Tina Trettin

Printed in the United States of America

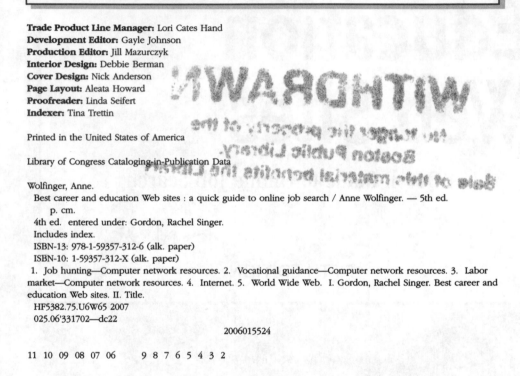

Library of Congress Cataloging-in-Publication Data

Wolfinger, Anne.
   Best career and education Web sites : a quick guide to online job search / Anne Wolfinger. — 5th ed.
      p. cm.
   4th ed. entered under: Gordon, Rachel Singer.
   Includes index.
   ISBN-13: 978-1-59357-312-6 (alk. paper)
   ISBN-10: 1-59357-312-X (alk. paper)
   1. Job hunting—Computer network resources. 2. Vocational guidance—Computer network resources. 3. Labor market—Computer network resources. 4. Internet. 5. World Wide Web. I. Gordon, Rachel Singer. Best career and education Web sites. II. Title.
   HF5382.75.U6W65 2007
   025.06'331702—dc22

                                        2006015524

11 10 09 08 07 06   9 8 7 6 5 4 3 2

We have been careful to provide accurate information throughout this book, but it is possible that errors and omissions have been introduced. Please consider this in making any important decisions. Trust your own judgment above all else and in all things.

Trademarks: All brand names and product names used in this book are trade names, service marks, trademarks, or registered trademarks of their respective owners.

Previous editions published as *Quick Internet Guide to Career and Education Information.*

ISBN-13: 978-1-59357-312-6
ISBN-10: 1-59357-312-X

Contents at a Glance

Contents

Career Exploration Information   63

Finding and Applying for Job Openings   87

Career Clearinghouses   111

8 Self-Employment and Small Business 147

9 Temporary Work, Contract Employment, Freelancing, Teleworking, and Volunteering 165

About This Book

One of the biggest challenges we face as we enter the adult world is finding or choosing a career path that supports us financially, challenges us mentally, and helps us grow our unique talents. For many adults, this is an ongoing challenge as we make career shifts out of either choice or necessity.

This book is designed to help you take advantage of the Internet's powerful resources. You'll find the Web sites carefully selected and grouped to help you find the information you want. In most sections, you have a choice of Web sites to work with, so if you don't find what you want at one you can visit another. If you want to dig more deeply, we show you how.

Information is one piece of career decision-making, and an important one. But there's also you. You are a unique mix of abilities, interests, talents, imagination, dreams, and possibilities. You have a lot to contribute to your future, your family, your community, your profession, and the world in general. When you take charge of your career, you look at who you are, figure out what questions to ask, look for information to help you, and filter out the rest.

So take charge, take heart, and let us help you along the way.

Best wishes.

—Anne Wolfinger

INTRODUCTION

Internet Tips and Electronic Resumes

The Internet has revolutionized how we find information in today's world of choices. Career descriptions, college entrance requirements, financial aid facts, job openings in your hometown or across the world—it's all online (if you can find it).

Because the online world presents so many opportunities, it can be hard to figure out the best places to begin. That's why we've put together the very best career and education Web sites to let you use the Internet as a powerful tool in your career and education decisions. We've done the research for you by selecting and evaluating more than 350 sites.

Here's what we looked for. To be included in this book, sites have to offer quality information, the bulk of it free of charge. Sites primarily promoting fee-based services or products were, for the most part, excluded. Also, we like sites that explain what they are, usually with an "About us" link at the bottom of the page. Another biggie we looked for was a statement of the site's privacy policy, which is especially important if you provide any personal information (you'll read more about this in the sidebar "Protect Your Privacy"). Finally, we're not fond of ads, but cut the sites some slack if their content is good despite the distraction.

If you want to investigate further, we give you ideas for doing that, too. Not only do we talk about searching for additional career and education information online, we also point out when a Web site can lead you to further information and to other related sites, which many of them do.

Before we get started describing our sites, we'll tell you a little about finding and using information on the Internet, including tips for protecting your privacy. In addition, we cover the basics of how to create and use an electronic resume.

Realize first that "the Internet" is basically just a giant network of computers, all connected to allow people to communicate and to share and find information. The most common ways people use the Internet—and the ones we talk about in this book—include the following:

➡ **The World Wide Web (WWW or the Web).** The Web lets you access information on Web sites, which can include text, pictures, video, audio, and more. Most of the Internet resources discussed in this book are Web sites.

➡ **Electronic mail (e-mail).** E-mail lets you send written messages to friends, relatives, and potential employers and lets them easily reply to you. Your messages can make it across the building or across the ocean within minutes or even seconds. You can also send your resume and apply for jobs via e-mail. We'll talk more about that in the section "Using Electronic Resumes."

The World Wide Web

The World Wide Web is most often accessed through a piece of software called a *Web browser*, usually Internet Explorer or Netscape Navigator. (If you use an online service such as AOL, you also have the option of using its built-in Web browser.) Each lets you navigate the Web through a graphical user interface, using the mouse to point and click your way to the information you need.

The point-and-click nature of the Web works because of the use of *hypertext*. Hypertext documents on the Web contain *hyperlinks* (or *links*), which connect you to other related information. When you click a word, phrase, button, or image that contains a link, a new Web page comes up on the screen. You can then choose to continue along that line of information, go back to your original location, or go off in yet another direction.

Understanding Web Addresses

Web addresses (called *URLs,* or *Uniform Resource Locators*) point you to specific Web sites on the Internet. A Web address works just like a postal address, identifying where on the Internet that particular Web site "lives." Although these addresses at first look somewhat confusing, there is a logic to them. Let's take apart the address http://www.jist.com/books.shtm and examine it piece by piece to see how it is put together.

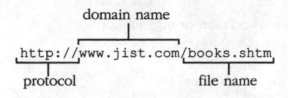

The beginning of any Internet address is the *protocol,* which tells the computer which part of the Internet you're using. For Web sites, you almost always see **http://**, which stands for Hypertext Transfer Protocol. Luckily, you don't need to type this part of the URL into a newer Web browser—it just assumes it's there.

www, which stands for *World Wide Web,* is often part of a Web address. Sometimes people leave it off when they talk about Web addresses (saying "jist.com" instead of "www.jist.com," for example). Just be aware that some URLs do not contain the www. For those sites, we've included the full URL with **http://** (such as http://mapping-your-future.org) so that you won't add the www and get lost. Also, variations are starting to pop up, such as "www2." Just type the Web address exactly as it appears in the book, and you will be fine.

jist.com is the *domain name.* It's basically the most important part of the Internet address; it gets you to the company, organization, or other entity that owns that domain. The part before the dot often is similar to the name of the company or other entity that owns the Web site. (In this case, "jist" stands for JIST Publishing.) The letters after the dot (the *extension*) identify what type of organization it is. Here are the most common extensions:

.com for a commercial site

.biz for companies

.edu for a university or educational institution

.gov for a government agency

.net for a network

.org for an association or organization

.mil for a branch of the U.S. Military

.info for an informational site

.name for individuals

To see all the different domain extensions, visit ICANN at www.icann.org. New extensions are being added to allow the Internet to continue to grow and develop, especially since the .com extension has become so overloaded. You can follow the discussions and arguments about when and why to add them at ICANN's Web site. Also note that you might run into even more extensions during your online travels. For example, each country is assigned a two-letter code. You'll see .ca for some Canadian sites, such as www.jobbank.gc.ca. However, most U.S. Web sites prefer to use .com, .org, and .edu.

books.shtm is the file name of the information you're viewing—the name of that file on the computer you are visiting on the Internet. The last part of the file name is usually htm, html, or shtml. (Sometimes you see newer file names that end in .asp or another group of letters, but just type them in exactly as you see them.) *htm* and *html* mean *Hypertext Markup Language,* the language of the Web; an *shtml* file is just an html file that uses a slightly different technology. As with word-processing or spreadsheet files, you can copy, print, or save an htm, html, or shtml file.

Those are the basics of Web addresses. Of course, they can be much longer than our example because of the complexity of content on a Web site. You often see directory paths between the domain name and file name, located between slashes. Directory paths just tell the host computer where to look for the file you want. A Web address can also specify a location within a file (a section farther down the page, for example) or show the results of search criteria you've entered.

The Power of Portals

Some people like to set a favorite search engine as their browser's home page so that they can quickly start looking for the information they need every time they go online. Many search engines and directories have transformed into portals that let you view your local news, weather, e-mail, and more on the same page you search from. Therefore, using one as your home page can be handy (and simple to set up—most search engines help you do it in one or two clicks).

Search-engine portals can be powerful, time-saving tools in your job search. From a single Web site, they allow you to do the following:

- Get a free e-mail address. You can use this address just for your job search, to keep your personal and business correspondence separate.
- Locate employer contact information through links to online white pages and yellow pages.
- Find your way to an interview. Use the mapping feature on some portal pages (such as Yahoo!) to map the route from your house to the interview, and then print it for take-along convenience.
- Stay informed. You can personalize your portal and have it deliver news, stock reports, and more based on the demographic data and preferences you provide when you register.
- Prepare for the inevitable job interview small talk by reading late-breaking head-lines right on your search-engine page.
- Figure out how to dress for tomorrow's interview (and how much time to allow to get there) by checking the local weather forecast.

Searching the Web

Search engines and directories are special Web sites that have indexed large portions of the Internet. They allow you to specify the information you are looking for, and then they bring up a list of Web sites, or pages from Web sites, that meet your criteria. Although Web browsers such as Netscape Navigator and Internet Explorer include a Search option on their toolbars, there are many other ways to search. We'll talk about some of the options next.

But first, let's look at the basics of successful Internet searching:

1. Pick your topic. The first step is to identify what you want to research and to define it as specifically as possible.

2. Pick your search engine. Different search engines can be better for different types of topics, or for broader as opposed to very specific searches, so your topic can influence which search engine you use. In the next sections we'll talk more about different types of search engines and directories and when to use each.

3. Type in two or three words, or *keywords,* to tell the search engine what you're looking for.

Boolean Logic

Many search engines use *Boolean logic,* named after nineteenth-century mathematician George Boole, who invented it. Boolean logic uses the terms AND and OR. An AND search means that the search engine will turn up only the results that contain *both* items or terms you have listed. An OR search means you'll settle for either one. Nine times out of ten, an OR search gives you a bigger list.

For example, I did a simple search on Google for **librarian AND salaries** and got 1,830,000 results. Searching for **librarian OR salaries** produced 144,000,000 results. My best search results resulted from typing in **"librarian salaries"** with quotation marks, which tells Google to look for that specific phrase. This search returned 13,600 results, many of which looked promising.

Search engines may simplify matters for you. Look for an "advanced search" link or button, which usually produces a list of search choices for you, like **all the words, the exact phrase, any of the words,** or **none of the words.** Other options may include language, date, or domain type.

Consider investing a little time in becoming an expert searcher by checking out some online tutorials. See the section "More Search Options" for some places to start.

The two main varieties of search engines are Internet directories and indexed search engines. Some, however, combine both types on the same site for extra searching power, and others have morphed themselves into multifeatured personalized portal sites. (See the earlier sidebar "The Power of Portals.")

When deciding which type of search engine to use, consider what you're looking for. Directories are handy for exploring a general concept or broad, open-ended questions. Browsing through a list of categories might alert you to related topics you hadn't previously considered. Indexed search engines are best for a more narrowly defined topic.

Internet Directories

Internet directories organize Web sites into categories that let visitors drill down from broad to very specific topics. For example, let's say you wanted to use Yahoo!, the best-known Internet directory, to get a list of sites that provide information on the federal minimum-wage law. You could drill down through the categories as follows: Business and Economy: Employment and Work: Employment and Workplace Issues: Minimum Wage. Directories usually aim to provide just the "best" sites in each category, rather than creating a comprehensive index of as many Web sites as possible.

Many Internet directories also give you the option of doing a keyword search, but beware: They might be searching just their own directories and not the entire Web. Or, if they do include the rest of the Web in their search, their directory sites might get top billing over other Web sites. How do you know? Sometimes they tell you, but for the behind-the-scenes story, visit the Search Engine Showdown Web site at www.notess.com/search/, which is described in the section "Further Search Help."

Here are a couple examples of Internet directories:

Open Directory Project
http://dmoz.org

> The Netscape-administered Open Directory Project (ODP), the largest human-edited Web directory, is maintained entirely by volunteer editors around the world. Editors are responsible for selecting, organizing, updating, and annotating the links in their own categories. (Are you an expert on a subject? Consider signing up to help!) Unlike some other directories, ODP never charges to list URLs. On the downside, the quality of different categories can be inconsistent. Several major search engines use ODP data to power their own directories.

Yahoo!

www.yahoo.com

Search or drill down through the Yahoo! categories, or personalize your own Yahoo! home page to include access to e-mail, an appointment calendar, local weather, headline news, and more. Click Help for search tips and other information on using and personalizing the site. With a simple click or two, you can also make Yahoo! your home page.

Those Annoying Ads

Okay, we admit it. We don't like ads. However, they are a growing fact of life on the Internet, especially for Web sites that rely on advertising to support their content and services. Ads range from the rather unobtrusive Google text ads to pop-ups, pop-unders, and, the most distracting, action ads. Web technology can track your linking activity, and sophisticated Web sites can tailor the information, especially the advertising, you see based on it.

Here are some suggestions to help you keep your ad exposure under control:

- You can choose whether to use ad-laden sites. Chances are excellent that you can find another site with the information or services you're looking for. We refuse to use sites with *pop-under ads*, which appear after you exit the site.

- *Pop-up blockers*, as their name implies, can prevent pop-up ads that appear on some sites and force you to click through them to get to what you really want. If you download the Yahoo! toolbar, for example, you also get a pop-up blocker.

- *Ad-aware software* detects and removes behavior-tracking spyware, data mining, aggressive advertising tactics, and tracking components. The personal version is available free of charge from www.lavasoft.com.

Indexed Search Engines

Indexed search engines vary in what they cover and how they categorize sites, but each uses computerized indexing rather than humans to index Web sites and then allows visitors to search through that index for information of interest.

To understand why you receive different results from each search engine, realize that some search engines index the entire contents of a Web page. Others index only specific parts, such as the title or top heading, or hone in on keywords that the Web page author embeds at the top of the page (inside a *metatag*) to describe that page's content. For example, some of the keywords for jist.com are resumes, job search, career, jobs, books, videos, reference, workbooks, assessments, and cover letters. Each applies to the types of material JIST publishes.

Each search engine also uses different criteria to rank Web sites, so one of the top sites to show up in one search engine might appear far down the list—or not at all—in another. These rankings can depend on how often your keyword appears on a particular Web page, how popular that page is (for example, how often it is linked to from other Web sites), or a number of other factors, including advertising. "Sponsor" sites pay fees to appear at the top of search lists.

Keyword searches are common, and you'll find them not only in search engines, but also within many Web sites. Many of the job banks described in chapter 4, for example, offer a keyword search to help you sort through their job listings.

Not only do search engines index the Internet differently, but each displays your results in different ways. Some, for example, show you the total number of pages found. Others display just the titles of the pages. Still others provide annotations from their partner directory or descriptions provided by the Web page creators themselves.

As mentioned in the sidebar "Boolean Logic," many search engines offer you the choice of doing simple or advanced searches. Advanced searching usually gives you more control. A good plan is to try a simple search first and see what happens and then switch to an advanced search if you are unhappy with your initial results.

Here are some examples of indexed search engines:

Google
www.google.com

Google's sense of humor is apparent in its name (a "googol" is a 1 followed by 100 zeroes, equal to 1.0^{100}) and in its penchant for decorating its logo to celebrate holidays and special occasions. Your search terms are highlighted within the results in an excerpt from that page, and sponsored links are clearly marked at the top and sides of results lists. Google also offers special searches for news, different file types, and a large number of advanced search options. Google offers a downloadable toolbar for Internet

Explorer so that you can do an instant Google search at any time without first going to the Google home page. You also can make Google your home page in a click or two. You can personalize your Google site and use any number of other Google services, including news alerts, blogging and blog searches, full-text book searches, mailing lists and discussion groups, and Google's version of e-mail.

Ask.com

www.ask.com

Download the Ask.com toolbar to quickly access Ask.com's powerful search engine, do a quick word lookup in the dictionary, or e-mail any Web page to a friend. Ask.com uses a unique search function that locates communities on the Web within their specific subject areas, producing search results that come with suggestions for narrowing or expanding your search. You can even install a desktop version of Ask.com to index the contents of your own computer, giving you high tech searching power closer to home— a big plus if you can't remember the file name or folder for your electronic resume. This site replaces Ask Jeeves.

More Search Options

Your other choices here usually allow you to go bigger (with metasearch engines that search a number of search engine databases at once) or smaller (with subject-specific or specialized databases). Metasearch engines can save time by searching a number of places at once, but it's harder to do an advanced search, because you don't have access to each site's tools. Smaller or subject-specific databases can let you do a more focused search when you need a very specific piece of information, such as a phone number. The Web has hundreds of search engines. To find more, try exploring the sites listed in the next section, or check out the Internet Search Engine database at www.isedb.com.

Dogpile

www.dogpile.com

Dogpile has "all the best search engines piled into one," including Google, Yahoo! Search, MSN Search, and Ask. Its front page offers options to search for Web pages, images, audio or video files, news, yellow pages (for companies), and white pages (for individuals). Search results indicate where the sites were found. Sponsored sites are clearly indicated. Advanced search options offer you more searching power. Download the Dogpile toolbar for quick desktop access.

Vivísimo

http://vivisimo.com

Another metasearch engine, Vivísimo searches a number of search engines and provides results both in a typical top-results list and in "clusters" of information. Clusters group results into several related subjects; you can choose any cluster to see the actual sites found. Each result shows the search engine(s) it came from, and you can click Preview to see a snippet of the site without having to load the whole page and move away from your results list. Advanced Search lets you specify which search engines to use and a number of advanced syntax options for more precise searching.

WhitePages.com

www.whitepages.com

At WhitePages.com, you can find a person, a phone number, an area code, a zip code, a toll-free number, maps, and more. It's an all-around useful little site. You can also do reverse searches, in which you enter a phone number and get an address. This can come in handy for those "blind" job ads.

Further Search Help

Search Engine Showdown
www.notess.com/search/

> Librarian Greg Notess provides this "users' guide to Web search-
> ing" to help you make the most out of your Internet searches.
> You'll find reviews of search engines, news, statistics, tutorials,
> feature comparisons, and more. Search Engine Showdown also
> compares and discusses the major Internet directories, news and
> phone number search engines, and other related sites. It's the
> place to start for information on all the major search engines.

The Spider's Apprentice
www.monash.com/spidap.html

> The Spider's Apprentice is "a helpful guide to Web search
> engines." Want to know how your favorite stacks up against the
> competition? In addition to answers to frequently asked questions
> and helpful search strategies, The Spider's Apprentice conducts in-
> depth analysis and rankings.

Web Search Strategies
www.learnwebskills.com/search/main.html

> For a straightforward tutorial on honing your Web searching skills,
> try Web Search Strategies from Internet training pro Debbie
> Flanagan. Complete with exercises, Web Search Strategies guides
> you step-by-step through the seemingly complicated world of
> search engines. You'll learn about using search engines, subject
> directories, metasearch engines, and specialty databases. It
> includes in-depth instruction on searching the most popular search
> engines, as well as practice searches to get you started.

E-mail

Electronic mail (e-mail) is the Internet's most popular feature—and for good reason. E-mail lets you stay in touch with everyone from friends to co-workers, sending messages nearly instantly within the office, across the street, or around the world.

E-mail is the most basic tool in your Internet job search. It's nearly impossible today to conduct an effective job search without e-mail, and it's impossible to do an effective Internet job search without having a handle on e-mail basics.

E-mail is important because it

➡ Allows employers to contact you quickly and easily

➡ Allows you to send your electronic resume to potential employers

➡ Allows you to receive notifications from personal job search agents (for more on job search agents, see chapter 4)

➡ Allows employers to see you as a technologically savvy applicant

➡ Allows you to network online with others in your field

E-mail software comes bundled with computer operating systems (such as Outlook in Windows) as well as in the software for online services such as America Online (AOL). You'll need an account from an Internet Service Provider (ISP) to use the e-mail software that comes with your computer or to use other free or commercial e-mail software you buy or download. (The two most popular free e-mail programs are Eudora, available at www.eudora.com, and Pegasus Mail, available at www.pmail.com.) You need information from your ISP to set up your e-mail software initially, but most walk you through the process over the phone in just a couple minutes. You can also sign up for free Web-based e-mail service on a number of Internet sites.

Protect Your Privacy

Any time you register at a Web site, download a toolbar or free software, subscribe to a free e-newsletter, buy a product online, or post your resume, you expose yourself to a potential loss of some of your privacy. When you use the Internet, information is being gathered about you whether or not you know it (see the preceding sidebar, "Those Annoying Ads").

Get smart about your privacy. Here are some suggestions:

- Look for a statement of a Web site's privacy policy, and read it. In particular, look for information on who the site shares user data with. If you can opt out of information sharing, do so.

- Be careful each time you are asked for personal information on a Web site. Complete only the required information, and, depending on the site, even consider fudging on the truth.

- Be selective as to the number of sites you register with. The more times you provide your name, e-mail address, and other information, the greater your exposure to spam and unwanted junk mail.

- Never respond to an e-mail asking you to "update" your personal information, especially financial info. Phishing is an Internet scam that attempts to collect private user information to be used for identity theft. You receive an e-mail directing you to an authentic-looking Web site, where you are asked to update personal information, such as passwords and credit card, Social Security, and bank account numbers. A legitimate Web site or organization would already have these.

- Control your cookies. A cookie is a text-only string that gets entered into your browser's memory. Cookies allow Web sites to personalize information, help with online sales or service, or collect demographic information. You can find out more about cookies and how to set your browser to control them at Cookie Central, www.cookiecentral.com/faq/.

- Use free e-mail to be ultra-selective about who you give your "main" e-mail address to, or use a free address temporarily as a place to receive job notices.

E-mail Addresses

E-mail addresses, like Web site addresses, provide a standard way to locate someone on the Internet. They are put together in a fairly straightforward manner that makes sense when you understand what each part of the e-mail address does. Let's take a typical e-mail address and look at each part of it:

info@jist.com

The first part of an e-mail address (**info**) is the user name, which identifies a unique mailbox. You can usually pick your own user name, but on big Web-based e-mail providers, or online services such as AOL, so many people are using e-mail that you might have to add numbers or letters to make your user name unique. (This is how people end up with e-mail addresses with user names like "joezzz" and "fred123.")

Every e-mail address includes the **@** symbol. This is how you know it is an e-mail address rather than a Web site or another Internet address.

The part after the @ sign is the domain name (**jist.com**). Just like the domain portion of a Web site address, this lets you know the company or organization that the e-mail address is part of.

Signature, Please!

Your e-mail *signature* is simply a little block of text that is automatically included at the bottom of each of your outgoing e-mail messages. It can include your name and contact information, a quote, a pitch, a tagline, or a message that sums up you and your qualifications.

Almost all e-mail software and Web-based e-mail allow you to create a signature. Why not make yours useful to employers and show your enthusiasm? A job seeker might try something like this on outgoing cover letters:

Looking forward to putting my five years of (specific work experience) to work for you.

Or:

Member, (name of job-related professional associations to which you belong)

Put your contact information in your signature to make sure you don't forget to include it in the e-mail cover letters you send. Get creative if you want. Test it. But be sure to keep your signature brief and professional. Don't impose on readers by including huge quotes that are longer than your e-mail message itself, for example.

Free Web-Based E-mail

In addition to free e-mail software packages such as Eudora and Pegasus mail, a number of companies and Web sites now offer free Web-based e-mail service.

So what's in it for them? These Internet companies provide you free e-mail in return for your demographic information, which is valuable to them and their advertisers. You get the service for free, but you have to look at ads every time you use your online e-mail box. Some even e-mail you advertising in addition to the banner ads and other advertisements you see on the Web pages you use to access your e-mail. Check the site's privacy policy and opt out of such advertising if you can.

So what's in it for you? Web-based e-mail services allow you to read and send e-mail from any Internet-connected computer—at the library, at home, at work, at school, or at a friend's house. It also provides you with a consistent e-mail address: Even if you change ISPs and lose your e-mail address with your provider, your Web-based address stays the same. If you share an Internet account with others in your family, you can use Web-based e-mail to set up a private e-mail address. Some of these e-mail providers also include calendars and other add-ons to make Web-based e-mail even more useful.

You can use the Free E-mail Providers Guide at www.fepg.net to locate the Web mail that is right for you, or check out the following two free Web-based e-mail providers:

MSN Hotmail

http://hotmail.msn.com

> In addition to a generous 250 MB of e-mail in-box storage, MSN Hotmail offers powerful spam filters and enhanced virus scanning and cleaning—important tools for keeping your computer healthy. With MSN Hotmail, you can also send up to 10 MB of files or byte-greedy photos.

Yahoo! Mail

http://mail.yahoo.com

> Yahoo! Mail scores high marks for its sophisticated security features, a configurable spam filter, and anti-virus scanning and cleaning. Yahoo! Mail was the first Web-based mail service to include a detailed address book, calendar, and notepad, and these work as well as ever. Yahoo! Mail is part of Yahoo!'s portal services.

E-mail Savvy

During your job search, you've probably spent a lot of time developing your network of contacts. Why spend time scrolling through hundreds of old e-mail messages trying to find someone's contact information or messages on a specific topic? Use the capabilities of your e-mail software or Web mail to get organized.

Common e-mail functions include

- Setting up mailboxes (or folders) to archive and organize old messages
- Saving and organizing e-mail addresses in an address book
- Saving the e-mail addresses of a group of people together, which helps you send a message to the group without having to type each individual address
- Sorting e-mails by status, priority, sender, date, subject, and so on
- Setting up filters to automatically direct incoming mail to a particular folder or mailbox
- Setting up filters to automatically open, copy, print, or delete a message

Taking a moment to read your program's manual or Help menu can save you time and help you organize your all-important e-mail. Now that's a win-win proposition!

E-mail Etiquette

 Be brief.

 Be professional. Avoid profanity, slang, and so on in any message to colleagues or a potential employer. If you wouldn't put it in a cover letter, don't include it in your e-mail message.

 Use the subject header effectively. Give the addressee a clue about the content of your message.

 Be selective. Send your message only to those who need to see it.

 Check your spelling. Most e-mail software now includes spell-check features.

Using Electronic Resumes

Today, creating an electronic resume is almost the same as creating a regular resume. You just need to create and save your resume in Microsoft Word or similar word-processing software and take a couple of steps to change it into other commonly requested formats. You're then ready to post it online or e-mail it directly to employers.

> **Note:** If you need help creating a resume, check out Susan Britton Whitcomb's *Résumé Magic,* Second Edition (JIST Publishing, 2003), or see the resume Web sites listed in chapter 4.

Types of Electronic Resumes

There are three common types of electronic resumes. This section explains how to create and when to use each.

→ **Microsoft Word.** You'll often see job ads requesting that candidates send their resume in "Word format." They are asking for a copy of the file you create when you type up and save your resume in Microsoft Word. If you use another word-processing program to create your resume, such as WordPerfect, don't worry. You can save most documents in Microsoft Word format. (Typically, all you have to do when saving your file is choose Save As from the File menu. Then select Microsoft Word from the options listed.)

→ **ASCII (or "plain-text") resumes.** ASCII resumes are the lowest common denominator of electronic resumes. Although they might look plain and boring, some employers prefer to receive this type of resume to help them scan more easily for keywords (see the next section) and to reduce their risk of catching a computer virus from Word resumes. The easiest way to create an ASCII resume is to open your Microsoft Word resume and select Save

As from the File menu. In the "Save as type" list, select Plain Text, and click Save. (Ignore any warnings Word gives you about losing formatting.)

Your resume is then saved as plain text. You can check by looking in the directory where you saved it. Your original resume will be listed as *resumename*.doc, and your text resume will be listed as *resumename*.txt.

Open your plain-text resume in a program such as Windows Notepad. Just double-click the name of the .txt file when you are looking at your directory. Notice that all the special formatting from your Word resume, such as bold, underline, and bullets, has been lost. You need to go through your text resume in Notepad and make it look as nice as possible without using any special formatting, because this is exactly how an employer will see your resume. When you're done, just resave it.

HTML (or "Web page") resumes. You can put your resume online in the form of a Web page. This allows you to do things such as include links from your resume to projects you have done, your e-mail address, and other useful information for employers. Putting your resume online as a Web page also allows employers to find you. This is easier than ever before because of user-friendly graphical Web page editing software such as Microsoft FrontPage and free Web hosting services such as Tripod.com. You can even use Microsoft Word to create a basic HTML resume by choosing Save As from the File menu and then choosing Web Page from the "Save as type" list. Also, ask whether your school allows students to post resumes online, which might help employers find you from your school's Web site.

One of the things to be especially careful about with your Web page resume is to keep it looking as professional as possible. Because it is so easy to add pictures, music, and so on to a Web page, sometimes people go overboard and make employers look at family photos and listen to songs. You don't want to distract anyone looking at your HTML resume from its main point: you and your qualifications.

Using Keywords

You will want to use *keywords* to make your resume match the terms used in employers' job ads as closely as possible. These kinds of keywords are different from those discussed earlier with search engines. Keywords in this sense are the "hot" words (usually nouns) that are associated with a specific industry, profession, or job function. Using keywords is especially important if you are applying to large companies, which might use a computer to search through all the resumes they receive and reject any that don't have the right keywords. The best way around this is to be sure to include keywords to get your resume past the first cut.

Luckily, you've already put your resume in electronic format. This makes it easy for you to make changes and use the precise keyword terms mentioned in the ads.

Always be as specific as possible. Read each job ad carefully, and be ready and willing to make changes to your resume when applying for different positions.

Getting Your Resume Online

There are a couple of different ways to get your resume online and in front of employers. The first (and easier) way is to respond to employers who ask for a copy of your Microsoft Word or plain-text resume via e-mail. (If you don't have an e-mail address yet, check out the section "Free Web-Based E-mail" for ideas on how to get a free one.)

Employers who want a Word resume will want it as an e-mail attachment. Any e-mail software program lets you attach a file to a message. Just write a message including your cover letter, and then select the option in your software or in your Web mail to attach a file. Browse to the place you have saved your resume, and select that file to attach to your e-mail message. It will be sent with the message so that the employer can open it and see it just as you saved it.

Employers who specify a plain-text resume will want it either as an attachment or inside the e-mail message itself. If they want it inside the message, first type your cover letter as an e-mail to the employer. Then open your plain-text resume in Notepad and use copy and paste to include the text of your resume right under your cover letter.

The next way to get your resume online is to post it in a resume bank on one of the major job boards, such as Monster. (You'll find information on a bunch of these in chapter 4.) When you see the option to post your resume online, you usually get a form to fill out. Again, use copy and paste to transfer information from your resume into this form.

Using your resume electronically saves you and employers time, lets you tailor each resume for the specific job opening, and shows potential employers that you have some computer know-how. Many of the Web sites in this book give you the opportunity to use your electronic resume, so have it ready to go.

CHAPTER 1

College and Financial Aid Information

We place great value on higher education—and with good reason. Higher education can bring a number of benefits, from career satisfaction to personal enhancement. However, the advantage that stands out the most is increased earning potential.

Take a look at these numbers. The U.S. Census Bureau reported in 1993 that the average wage for a college graduate working full-time was $28,068, or $15,108 higher than that of a high school graduate. Ten years later, college grads on average earned $51,206, or $23,291 more than high school grads—a million dollars more over the course of a 43-year career.

The lifelong increased earning potential for college graduates is a persuasive argument for a college education, but getting into and through college can be a job in itself. Fortunately, a number of Web sites can help you get started with planning for college, choosing a school, and funding your education. An investigation of them will save you or someone you love (and support) time and trouble as you begin your adventures in higher education.

Researching Colleges

These Web sites are the best places to begin looking for school-specific information. Most of them use a search tool to help you find what you're looking for. The number and types of schools they cover vary from site to site, as the descriptions show, so if you don't find what you're looking for at one, try another. Several also include information on financial aid, getting into schools, and much more, so spend some time browsing to see what is available.

CampusTours.com

www.campustours.com

"Virtual" college tours here range from straightforward online videos about a school to 360-degree panoramic images. Extras include maps, photos, webcams, and links to university Web sites. To take full advantage of CampusTours, make sure you have the latest versions of the QuickTime, Flash, Windows Media Player, RealPlayer, and IPIX plugins—all of which can be downloaded and installed from this site. Take the opportunity to view what each campus has to offer without having to travel.

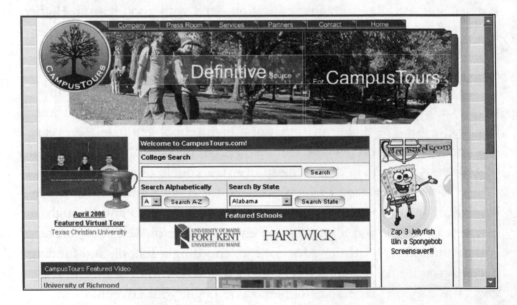

Community College Web

www.mcli.dist.maricopa.edu/cc

Community College Web is a searchable index of close to 1,300 community college Web sites in the U.S., Canada, and around the world. It also has many links to other community college-related resources. Use the search form to find colleges' Web sites by name, location, or keyword. The site is maintained by the Maricopa Center for Learning and Instruction of the Maricopa Community Colleges system in Arizona.

GradSchools.com

www.gradschools.com

As the name implies, GradSchools.com lists only graduate school programs, but there are more than 58,000 of them. Select from a lengthy alphabetical list of programs, or choose your preferred part of the country. Online graduate programs are also listed. Your search results show the degrees each institution offers, with contact information and a Web link for more information.

myFootpath.com

www.myfootpath.com

The folks at myFootpath.com call themselves "experts in college admissions," and you'll find a lot of information on the process here. Read Q&A articles in the Ask the Counselor section, browse articles on college preparation and college life, and sign up for a free e-mail newsletter. If you have a particular school in mind, you can also purchase inside admissions reports on specific colleges to get in-depth information on the application process.

Petersons.com

www.petersons.com

Peterson's is best known for its test-preparation and admissions guides, but it provides a generous amount of free information on this extensive site. Search for colleges, nursing programs, culinary schools, visual and performing arts schools, and more. Get contact information and find ways to apply online, or visit the schools' own sites for further information. If you're just beginning the college application process, Peterson's can help you get organized with the free, monthly Getting In! Planner e-newsletter.

The Princeton Review

www.princetonreview.com

Search the Princeton Review's Web site database for colleges, business schools, law schools, medical schools, graduate schools, or graduate programs. If you're uncertain in which direction to go, try the Princeton Review career quiz, which matches careers to your work style. Helpful articles provide a variety of information on admissions, testing, and financial aid. While visiting, also work on your test-taking skills with free online practice tests (SAT, ACT, and more) after you register. Or search the scholarship and financial aid database and store your results for future reference.

RWM Vocational School Database

www.rwm.org/rwm

This handy little site provides contact information for private post-secondary vocational schools in all 50 states, including private schools that offer certificate, bachelor's, master's, and doctorate degrees in various academic, business, trade, and technical disciplines. Schools must be state-accredited or licensed. The database is organized by state and then by 22 vocational training fields, ranging from aircraft to welding.

U.S. Universities

www.usuniversities.com

> U.S. Universities allows you to search by state and/or degree program. Each listing contains contact information, a description of the school, and a listing of its programs, as well as a link to e-mail the university for more information. The site also contains a useful section on studying abroad, which you can search by country and/or subject. The site has separate directories for volunteer and teaching opportunities, overseas jobs, high school students interested in foreign programs, and overseas internships.

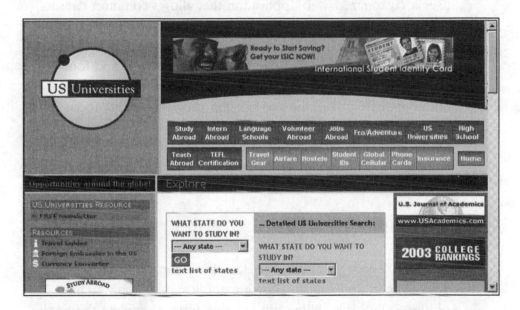

Web U.S. Higher Education

www.utexas.edu/world/univ

> This directory provides links to U.S. universities and community colleges that are regionally accredited. You can browse the list alphabetically or by state. Updated monthly, What's New shows the latest changes to the list. This site is simple and straightforward.

Apply Online!

Many individual schools let you apply online, but the following sites let you complete common application information and reuse it for multiple applications—saving you time and typing.

CollegeNET

www.collegenet.com

> CollegeNET lets you complete, file, and pay for admissions applications over the Internet for over 1,500 colleges and universities. It uses a customized Web application that allows common data to travel automatically from form to form, saving you time when filling out forms. To help you figure out where to apply, CollegeNET provides direct access to searches for national two- and four-year schools, vocational/technical and business schools, upper-level undergraduate programs, and nursing programs. Read about tuition, contact information, deadlines, and admission requirements, and then choose your type of application. Financial aid links and a scholarship search help you find funding after you apply.

Common Application

www.commonapp.org

> Nearly 300 colleges and universities have chosen to standardize the common application, allowing applicants to apply to any of these schools by filling out just one form. Complete the application online or download and print the form in .pdf (Adobe Acrobat—www.adobe.com) format. You can also find brief information on each participating school and a link to its Web site and e-mail address.

Getting the Scoop on College Entrance Exams

So you've finally narrowed it down to your top few choices—but don't forget that most schools require you to take one or more entrance exams. The following sites help you find out about common tests, register for them, and sign up for test-preparation courses online. Note that some sites mentioned earlier in this chapter, such as Petersons.com and The Princeton Review, are also good sources of testing information and resources.

ACT
www.actstudent.org/index.html

> Learn what to do before, during, and after taking the ACT, one of the most commonly required examinations for college applicants. You can register online, receive your scores online, learn how scores are reported, register to retake the exam, and have your results sent to additional schools. You can purchase an online test preparation program or book, or take advantage of the free booklets, sample tests, test descriptions, and test tips. Besides test-taking advice, there's information on financial aid, college, and career planning.

College Board
www.collegeboard.com

> Register online for the SAT, PSAT/NMSQT, CLEP, and AP exams. Exam descriptions and sample test questions help you prepare for the tests, or you can purchase test-taking software or books. Students with disabilities can find out about requesting accommodations for certain tests in the section "Services for Students with Disabilities (SSD)." Additional information on this site helps you plan for college, choose a school, and find out about financial aid options. This site also comes in a Spanish-language version.

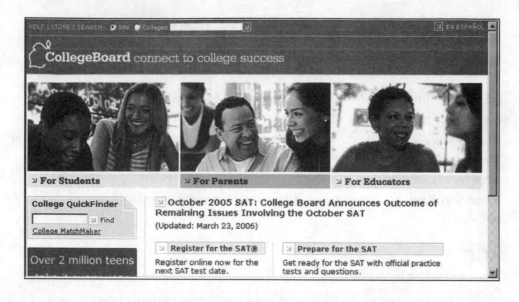

ETS (Educational Testing Service)

www.ets.org

At ETS, you can quickly link to information on popular tests like the GRE, SAT, and AP exam, or the Teaching of English as a Foreign Language (TOEFL) exam. If testing is in your future, try some sample questions online. Whether you're a student, parent, educator, researcher, or policymaker, ETS has some suggested resources for you.

FairTest: The National Center for Fair and Open Testing

www.fairtest.org/univ/optional.htm

The secret is out: Over 700 colleges and universities nationwide admit a substantial number of students without regard for their ACT or SAT test score. You can find every one of these schools at this site. The list includes a wide variety of institutions, from small, private liberal arts colleges to large, public university systems. Some of the schools require all applicants to submit test scores whether or not they use the test scores to make admissions decisions. The complete state-by-state list indicates to what extent the schools use the admissions tests, which some studies have shown to be inaccurate predictors of college success.

Kaplan: Test Prep and Admissions
www.kaptest.com

> For years, Kaplan has been known for its test-preparation courses. At kaptest.com, you can sign up to take onsite or online test preparation courses for entrance exams (for a fee), or take advantage of the site's free services. You'll see sample test questions, a variety of e-mail newsletters, and articles on applying to, paying for, and succeeding in college.

Your Money's Worth: College Rankings

U.S. News & World Report each year ranks the best colleges and graduate programs in a number of categories. A number of other magazines and Web sites have begun creating their own similar rankings. Although these are always somewhat subjective, rankings are a starting point to help you identify good schools to investigate further.

College and University Rankings (UIUC)
www.library.uiuc.edu/edx/rankings.htm

> The Education and Social Science Library at the University of Illinois Urbana-Champaign (UIUC) provides a large list of categorized links to college rankings, from undergraduate institutions to law schools. Even better, the site discusses how to understand and interpret the rankings so that you know how much weight to give them. Use this site to locate lists of colleges that are a best value, disability-friendly schools, and more.

USNews.com Education
www.usnews.com/usnews/edu/eduhome.htm

> Known for its rankings, *U.S. News* presents several of them here: rankings for universities and liberal arts colleges by region; graduate school rankings for several fields, including business, law, medicine, and public affairs; and best-value rankings. Access to

some of the information is restricted unless you pay a fee, but there's still plenty of good stuff for free, including college planner worksheets, a searchable scholarship database, a personality quiz, a college tuition planner, a loan repayment calculator, online forums where you can connect with others, and more.

Money Matters

Scholarships, loans, and savings plans are all important components of paying for a college education. The following sites help you identify your financial aid options—and, if it's early enough, get started with saving. Many also include additional information on choosing, applying to, and getting through school.

Adventures In Education

http://adventuresineducation.org

Sponsored by the Texas Guaranteed Student Loan Corporation, Adventures In Education provides information in English and Spanish for prospective college students. Helpful worksheets,

Internet links, and clear instructions help you choose and apply to schools, pay for college, select a career path, find a job after graduation, and manage your money. If you're planning on attending college soon, a handy financial aid calendar keeps you from overlooking important dates in the application process.

America's CareerInfoNet: Scholarship Search

www.acinet.org/acinet/scholarshipsearch/

One of the many tools in America's CareerInfoNet (see chapter 3 for more) is this database of over 5,000 scholarships, fellowships, loans, and other financial aid opportunities. Start with the Scholarship Search Help for pointers on using the system, which requires no registration or fee. The scholarship information comes from the Gale Group, which has a reputation for information excellence.

College Answer

www.collegeanswer.com

Get a head start on preparing for the world of continuing education through this Web site from Sallie Mae. Step-by-step instructions for students (and parents) in English or Spanish walk you through the college selection, application, decision, and financing process. Other helpful tools include an easy-to-use family of calculators for savings, budgeting, and loan repayment, and a school affordability analyzer.

College Is Possible

www.collegeispossible.org

College Is Possible is a national education campaign by the Coalition of America's Colleges and Universities to help address concerns about funding a college education for youth who are underrepresented in postsecondary education. Find out what educational institutions in your state participate in the program. Information here includes how to prepare for, choose, and pay for college, with a special section geared toward adult students.

College Savings Plans Network

www.collegesavings.org

All 50 states offer the 529 college savings plan (named after the part of the IRS code that authorizes them), and this site links to information on each state's unique programs. You'll find out about the 529 savings program, which allows families to put aside federal tax-exempt savings for college or purchase prepaid, locked-in tuition to state schools. The College Savings Plans Network was formed in 1991 as an affiliate to the National Association of State Treasurers to make higher education more attainable.

eStudentLoan.com

www.estudentloan.com

You need to register to use this free service, which allows you to search for both private and government loan programs. Follow the step-by-step guide to see what types of programs you qualify for, and then request applications or even apply online. eStudentLoan provides information on each loan, such as APR, fees, term, and average monthly payment, giving you the facts you need to make an informed decision.

FAFSA on the Web

www.fafsa.ed.gov

The Free Application for Federal Student Aid, fondly known as the FAFSA, is required for any student who wants federal assistance. The process is not speedy, but the site does an excellent job of laying out the steps to take, in English or Spanish. The hardest part may be gathering the financial information you need before you begin, like income tax return and bank statements, but the site lists all of those for you. Even better, the online application process lets you store your partially completed form so that you can finish it later if you're missing some required information. You can get your application processed the fastest by submitting it online, which requires obtaining an electronic personal identification number (PIN). Again, instructions here tell you how.

FastWeb

www.fastweb.com

FastWeb is one of the most reputable Internet scholarship search services. However, you must enter extensive information about yourself if you want to use it, including your age, mailing address, ethnicity, career objectives, academic background, student activities, and your parents' activities. The site uses this data to generate a personalized suite of information on colleges, internships, jobs, and scholarships, which number over 1.3 million and are worth over $3 billion. FastWeb is a Monster company.

Federal Student Aid

www.studentaid.ed.gov

For the official word on student financial assistance, turn to this site from the U.S. Department of Education. Organized in a very user-friendly manner to help you find the information you need, the site walks you through the financial steps of preparing, choosing, applying, funding, attending, and repaying. Learn where to begin whether you are in elementary school, junior high, high school, college, or graduate school, or if you are a returning student, international student, parent, or counselor. Information here includes descriptions of the different federal student aid programs and eligibility requirements, help in choosing your ideal college, a financial aid wizard to help calculate your college costs, and much more. Learn about the process for applying online for financial aid, and then go do it at FAFSA on the Web (described a couple of paragraphs ago). Last but not least, the information here on repaying, consolidating, or finding forgiveness programs for existing loans is useful for graduates.

FinAid!

www.finaid.org

Established in 1994, this award-winning site remains the most comprehensive online clearinghouse on funding a college education. Choose from loans, scholarships, military aid, and other types of aid to learn about all your options, and then check out extra tools such as links to financial aid applications, calculators, and personalized advice. FinAid! is now part of Monster.

Hispanic Scholarship Fund (HSF)

www.hsf.net

HSF is the nation's leading organization supporting Hispanic higher education. HSF was founded in 1975 with a vision to strengthen the country by advancing college education among Hispanic Americans—the largest minority segment of the U.S. population. Since then, HSF has awarded more than 73,000 scholarships totaling nearly $170 million to Latinos from all 50 states who have attended 1,700 colleges and universities. The site provides information on scholarship eligibility, application, and selection.

Mapping Your Future

http://mapping-your-future.org

Although Mapping Your Future provides information on the career-planning process, the main focus of this site is selecting and paying for college. Get started by taking a guided tour based on your category—middle or high school student, undergraduate, adult student, parent, counselor, and so on. Special features include online loan counseling interviews, financial fitness guides and calculators, scheduled interactive chat sessions on financial aid topics, and information on selecting and working toward a career. For more local information, check out the list of sponsors to see if there is a link to an agency in your state. This site is in both English and Spanish.

MyRichUncle

https://www.myrichuncle.com

If you can't cover the cost of your education through financial aid or parental aid, learn about private lending from MyRichUncle. Get informed about things like APR, origination fees, and capitalization, and then decide if a private loan should be part of your school finance plan. If you like what you see, you can apply online for private, internship, or study-abroad loans.

Nellie Mae

www.nelliemae.com

Nellie Mae, a wholly owned subsidiary of SLM Corporation (Sallie Mae, described next), allows you to apply or prequalify online for student loans. In many cases it provides an instantaneous response. You'll learn about the different types of loans that are offered, including requirements, fees, interest rates, and repayment options. Calculators help you compare award letters, set up a budget, calculate accrued interest on unsubsidized loans, compute prepayment savings, and more. The EDvisor Debt Management section can help you keep track of your payments, especially if you take out multiple loans.

Sallie Mae

www.salliemae.com

Sallie Mae, the leading provider of education loans, primarily funds federally guaranteed student loans. Here you can find information to help you prepare for, select, apply to, and finance college. The online Entrance Counseling Quiz tests your knowledge of student loans and may fulfill the entrance-counseling requirement at your school. Manage Your Loans is a useful resource tool that lets you review your account, keep your personal information current, make payments, and more.

ScholarshipHelp.org

www.scholarshiphelp.org

Learn the ins and outs of applying for a variety of scholarship opportunities at ScholarshipHelp.org. Read up on college costs, college loans, types of scholarships, how scholarship applications are judged, personal assessments, evaluating scholarship opportunities, scholarship essays, letters of recommendation, scholarship renewals, and more. Although this site doesn't have a scholarship database, links are provided to several.

SuperCollege

www.supercollege.com

> SuperCollege is an independent publisher of books and resources on college planning, including this Web site. In addition to a scholarship search (after you register for free), you'll find features organized for high school, college, and graduate students, parents, adult students, and counselors. Submit your scholarship or admissions questions to the experts, read the answers to questions submitted by others, or subscribe to the free scholarship and admissions newsletters.

United Negro College Fund (UNCF)

www.uncf.org

> UNCF is the nation's largest, oldest, most successful, and most comprehensive minority higher education assistance organization. UNCF provides operating funds and technology enhancement services for 39 historically black colleges and universities, scholarships and internships for students at about 900 institutions, and faculty and administrative professional training. The searchable database includes scholarships from UNCF and other organizations. If you're a student at a UNCF member college, filling out a profile is optional but highly recommended.

Interstate Student Exchange Programs

The following boards and commission sponsor programs that allow students to pursue degrees (in specified majors) at out-of-state institutions at less than the normal out-of-state tuition. This can result in significant savings if you want to attend school in another state. If you just want to study elsewhere in the U.S. or Canada for a year, there's a site for that too.

Midwestern Higher Education Compact (MHEC) Midwest Student Exchange Program

http://msep.mhec.org

The Midwest Student Exchange Program of the Midwestern Higher Education Compact (MHEC) serves students from Kansas, Michigan, Minnesota, Missouri, Nebraska, North Dakota, and Wisconsin. Through the program, public institutions agree to charge students no more than 150 percent of the in-state resident tuition rate for specific programs; private institutions offer a 10 percent reduction on their tuition rates. The site lists more than 125 participating colleges and universities, plus you can search by type of degree and school. Locate contacts for the participating states, or download a PDF brochure with all the information.

National Student Exchange

www.nse.org

If you long to expand your horizons but studying abroad is beyond your reach, check out the National Student Exchange. The program helps students study in other parts of the U.S. and Canada for up to one academic year. Students pay either their normal tuition and fees at the home campus or the in-state tuition and fees at their host campus. Since the program began nearly 40 years ago, over 80,000 students have used the program to broaden their academic careers.

New England Board of Higher Education (NEBHE) Tuition Assistance

www.nebhe.org/explain.html

If you're a resident of Connecticut, Maine, Massachusetts, New Hampshire, Rhode Island, or Vermont, the New England Regional Student Program (RSP) might save you money. Sponsored by the New England Board of Higher Education (NEBHE), the RSP provides a tuition break for students to study certain majors (that are not available at public colleges in their own states) at public colleges and universities in other New England states. Majors at all levels of study and participating institutions are listed in each year's RSP catalog, which you can download. You can also search the online database of programs and participating institutions.

Southern Regional Education Board (SREB) Academic Common Market

www.sreb.org/programs/acm/acmindex.asp

Through the Southern Regional Education Board (SREB) Academic Common Market program, residents can pursue unique majors at regional public institutions outside their home states while paying in-state tuition. You can even take distance courses through the SREB's Electronic Campus (described in chapter 2) under certain conditions, explained here. You also find out about the SREB Regional Contract Program, which gives out-of-state tuition breaks to students pursuing professional health degrees in fields such as dentistry and optometry. SREB's 16 member states are Alabama, Arkansas, Delaware, Florida, Georgia, Kentucky, Louisiana, Maryland, Mississippi, North Carolina, Oklahoma, South Carolina, Tennessee, Texas, Virginia, and West Virginia. Check the SREB Web site for more information, including contacts for specific programs in each state.

Western Interstate Commission for Higher Education (WICHE) Student Exchange Programs

www.wiche.edu/SEP

Students in Alaska, Arizona, California, Colorado, Hawaii, Idaho, Montana, Nevada, New Mexico, North Dakota, Oregon, South Dakota, Utah, Washington, and Wyoming can participate in this exchange program, which offers significant savings on out-of-state tuition among these Western states. Undergraduates, graduate students, and professional students can find out if their field of study is supported, find a list of schools, and learn how to apply.

General Information on Postsecondary Education

You'll find even more information on all aspects of postsecondary education at the next few sites.

Back to College

www.back2college.com

> If you're an adult entering college for the first time or you want to finish that degree you started years ago, this site is for you. Back to College contains information and links to topics from admissions to financial aid to finding a program. "Ask the Experts" your questions about going back to college, or talk with other returnees in the online forums. You can also sign up for a free monthly e-mail newsletter. Check out the site map for an organized breakdown of the subjects covered.

The Center For All Collegiate Information

www.collegiate.net

> The Center For All Collegiate Information is a comprehensive portal that serves as a one-stop directory for all aspects of postsecondary education. Sponsored by Aphco International, this Web site organizes college-related sites into areas from financial aid to graduate programs to distance-learning opportunities. Its slogan is "Bringing the collegiate world together on-line."

HEATH Resource Center

www.heath.gwu.edu

> George Washington University's HEATH Resource Center serves as a comprehensive clearinghouse on postsecondary education for students with disabilities. Browse the extensive links for annotated listings of related Web sites and organizations by topic areas, or read the quarterly newsletter and other free publications.

Students.gov

www.students.gov

Students.gov is a comprehensive information portal from the U.S. government on topics of interest to students. These include education, career development, military service, community service, and travel. The education sections provide links to choosing a college, testing, scholarships and grants, loan repayment, state financial aid, and more. Everything is searchable in case you're looking for something specific.

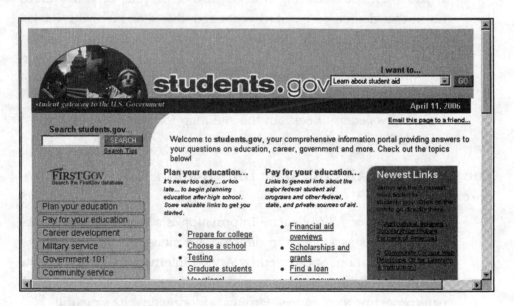

U.S. Department of Education

www.ed.gov/index.jhtml

Links on the main page of the U.S. Department of Education's Web site help you quickly locate information of interest to you, whether you are a student, parent, teacher, or administrator. You can get an overview of federal student aid, find links for planning for college or technical training, identify graduate student resources, locate information on studying abroad, and much more. You can also download popular publications such as the yearly Student Guide to Financial Aid. The site also offers education resources for Spanish speakers.

CHAPTER 2

Distance Learning and Lifelong Learning

Whether you want to complete a college degree or take a personal enrichment course, opportunities for learning without leaving your home continue to increase every year. *Distance learning* has become less novel and more mainstream for several reasons. Take improvements in technology, for example. Computers have gotten faster and less expensive, plus high-speed Internet access is now widely available and affordable.

More schools and institutions of higher learning are offering more courses, and they're getting better at it. In fact, the Distance Education Clearinghouse (described in this chapter) lists training programs for distance educators.

Ongoing learning is critical in the workplace, where employers face the need to maintain a well-trained staff and employees need to sharpen their skills to stay current or get ahead in their fields. For many, the availability and convenience of distance learning is hard to beat.

However, distance education carries a price tag (unless you're taking a free course at Barnes & Noble University, described in this chapter). Like any educational program, distance learning is an investment of your time and money. The Web sites in this chapter have been reviewed and selected to help you become a wise investor in distance learning.

Here are a few suggestions: Take the SORT assessment (described at the end of the next section) to help determine if distance learning is right for you. Search several sites to find the programs you're most interested in. No one directory lists all available programs. Do a little research on the employment outlook for the career you're exploring (see chapter 3) to be sure your investment can pay off. In my research, I spotted an online training course for TV/VCR repair—no doubt a declining occupation. Finally, be sure you know the total cost of your program of study. Some sites list costs by semester, and others by credit hour. Do the math yourself. Take advantage of any distance education advising a school or consortium offers prospective students to get the answers you need.

Learning About Distance Learning

Before you take the plunge, find out more about what you may be getting into. A little time spent investigating these sites can pay off in the long run.

About Distance Learning

http://distancelearn.about.com

About.com's distance learning section has a nice selection of general distance learning articles and resources—if you don't mind reading around ads that take up screen space. Articles on choosing a distance learning school, paying for school, and more are loaded with plenty of links for further research.

DegreeInfo.com

www.degreeinfo.com

DegreeInfo.com began as "a place where people genuinely interested in quality distance learning programs can come to discuss, learn, share, and help one another." The site started out as an active discussion board on distance learning, and that remains its outstanding feature. Read what others have to say about distance learning, or post a question yourself. In addition, the site has a searchable database of over 300 fully accredited schools.

Distance Education Clearinghouse

www.uwex.edu/disted/home.html

The University of Wisconsin–Extension provides the Distance Education Clearinghouse, a comprehensive, up-to-date directory of online resources on distance learning. Geared toward teachers, institutions, and students alike, its clearly annotated links are broken into a number of useful categories, including programs and courses, technology, teaching and learning, research and statistics, distance education community, and more. If you discover you really enjoy distance learning, there's a listing of certificate programs so that you can train to become an instructor yourself.

geteducated.com

www.geteducated.com/index.asp

Get educated about online education here. GetEducated.com's mission is to operate the only clearinghouse in the U.S. dedicated to showcasing accredited online degrees. Accreditation is important if you want a public record of your learning that will be widely accepted by employers, professional associations, and other colleges and universities. This site has surveys of top business and computer majors, "best buy" rankings for selected online programs, and free downloadable e-books listing accredited schools offering graduate and undergraduate degrees in specific areas.

University System of Georgia's Student Online Readiness Tool (SORT)

www.alt.usg.edu/sort/html/sortlau1.html

According to research, six main topics are closely related to a student's success in the online learning environment. SORT helps you rate yourself in each of these areas. Based on your responses to questions, you receive feedback on your personal readiness profile, along with suggested strategies for success and links to more information. Make this site a prerequisite before you sign up for any distance learning training.

Distance Learning Directories

Distance learning directories gather and organize distance learning offerings to make it easier for you to find what interests you.

Degree.net

www.degree.net

This companion Web site to Bears' Guide to Earning Degrees by Distance Learning and other distance learning guides includes columns, news stories, links to other distance education sites, and much more. Be sure to investigate the extensive accreditation information to get the background you need to evaluate distance learning schools and courses. This site also includes information on 100 recommended distance learning schools, listed alphabetically.

Distance.GradSchools.com

http://distance.gradschools.com

As you might guess from the name, this site specializes in distance learning graduate degrees. Distance graduate programs make it easier for adults with work and/or family responsibilities to earn graduate degrees from home, or by spending limited time on campus. Distance.Gradschools.com features a comprehensive list of programs of study and academic areas. Each school listing contains contact information as well as several links to the school's Web site for further information on the program.

Globewide Network Academy

www.gnacademy.org

If you think one distance learning directory is like another, think again. The Globewide Network Academy (GNA) focuses on research and developing Web technologies that promote distance learning and online communities. GNA lists certificate, continuing-education, and degree programs from preschool (no kidding) through postgraduate level. Nondegree courses are included as well. The site includes helpful articles, links, and information for those considering pursuing distance learning opportunities.

Petersons.com: Online Learning

www.petersons.com/distancelearning/

This page from Petersons.com provides an online search for hundreds of distance learning programs. You can search institutions by name, by degree programs, by degree programs without on-campus requirements, or by courses. You'll find detailed descriptions of most of the colleges, as well as contact information and links to their Web sites. See chapter 1 for more on Petersons.com.

USNews.com: Education: E-Learning

www.usnews.com/usnews/edu/elearning/elhome.htm

USNews.com's searchable e-learning directory includes more than 2,800 regionally accredited institutions offering distance course work for credit. Unlike most other directories, which require you to contact the school for financial information, USNews.com lists per-credit costs and the availability of financial aid for distance learning.

World Wide Learn

www.worldwidelearn.com

World Wide Learn has both online and on-campus directories, but since we're talking about distance learning, here's the scoop: World Wide Learn features both online degree programs and online nondegree courses. The degree programs are organized by type of degree, from high school through doctorate. Nondegree courses range from business skills and vocational training to foreign languages. So whether you're committed to a program or you just want to get your toes wet, this site is a good place to explore.

Distance Learning Career and Degree Institutions

This section offers a closer look at some institutions that offer distance learning programs. These examples show a nice range of possibilities, from high school diploma programs to vocational training to graduate degrees.

Center for Distance and Independent Study: University of Missouri–Columbia

http://cdis.missouri.edu/

Want an accredited four-year diploma—your high school diploma, that is? The Center for Distance and Independent Study of the University of Missouri–Columbia offers accredited high school courses for independent learners. Take courses online and apply the credit at your own high school, investigate classes not available in your area, catch up on courses, find courses for gifted students, supplement a home-schooling curriculum, or earn your diploma entirely online. If you qualify academically, you may even enroll in university-level courses offered through CDIS while paying only 50 percent of the normal University of Missouri educational fees. CDIS also offers middle-school courses and a bachelor of general studies degree program.

Jones International University

www.jonesinternational.edu

Jones International, the first accredited fully online university, offers undergraduate, graduate, and certificate programs with a focus on business. Its programs are developed and supported by content experts who are some of the most highly respected authorities in their fields. Each new student receives an online orientation to JIU, including instruction on using class Web pages and discussion forums, and peer and academic advisors are available via e-mail. JIU makes a strong effort to make education affordable, with several financial assistance programs and tuition payment options. It also offers credit for prior learning. This site is also available in Spanish.

Penn Foster Career School

www.pennfoster.edu

Penn Foster specializes in distance career programs for adult learners and offers a wide range of options, from child day care management to court reporter to motorcycle repair technician. Penn Foster also offers a high school degree program as well as associate's degrees in selected areas. Choose an area of interest to receive a free information packet by mail, and then enroll in a program to receive self-study materials at home. Proceed through modules and take exams online, by mail, or by phone at your own pace.

University of Phoenix

www.phoenix.edu

The nation's largest private university with over 115,000 students, the University of Phoenix gears its accredited graduate and under-graduate degree programs toward working adults. You can learn entirely online; take in-person courses near you at one of their 163 campuses across the U.S., Canada, Puerto Rico, and Mexico; or use a combination of both to complete your degree. Browse the site to find out about degrees offered, tuition costs, and financial aid.

University of Texas (UT)

www.telecampus.utsystem.edu

UT offers undergraduate degrees, master's degrees, and certificate programs, all online. You'll also find a searchable database of classes offered by any UT campus through any distance education method. Online professional development courses are available here as well. A good way to start is by reading the student hand-book, which you can find under Enrollment.

Walden University

www.waldenu.edu

Walden University offers programs in five academic areas: education, health and human services, management, psychology, and engineering and applied science. In addition, Walden's dual degree options allow you to expand the breadth of your learning and earn two degrees in less time than if you pursued each separately.

Western Governors University

www.wgu.edu/index.asp

Founded by the governors of several western states, Western Governors' program uses a unique competency-based (rather than credit-based) system. The programs are not based upon required courses. Instead, you earn your degree by demonstrating your competence through a series of carefully designed assessments—an approach that allows for extensive personalization. Program offerings include education, business, and information technology.

Distance Learning Consortia

State or regional distance learning consortia harness the power of multiple institutions to provide a broad array of classes and options to potential students, generally allowing students enrolled in one of the schools to take distance education courses at any other member institution. Again, these are just examples of the variety of consortia available. Find out whether your own state or regional board sponsors its own version.

Canadian Virtual University (CVU)

www.cvu-uvc.ca

The 12 universities in this consortium offer 280 complete degrees, diplomas, and certificates. More than 2,300 individual courses are available completely online or through distance education. Most, but not all, of the courses are open to international (non-Canadian) students. Search here for degree programs or for individual courses in your area of interest. Degrees are provided through your accredited "home university" rather than through CVU itself. This site is available in both English and French.

The College Network

www.college-net.com/

If you're an adult with work and life experience, take a look at the programs offered through the College Network. TCN works with its fully accredited partner institutions to help students earn up to 82 credits by testing out of prerequisites and general-education courses. Earn your associate's, bachelor's, or master's degree or professional certificate in less time than you anticipated.

Electronic Campus (Southern Regional Education Board)

www.electroniccampus.org/AdultLearner/

The Electronic Campus of the Southern Regional Education Board lists information on thousands of distance learning courses and programs for the 16 SREB states. (For more on SREB, see chapter 1.) Fortunately, the site also has powerful search tools to help you easily zoom in on your needs and interests. A number of courses are available at an "electronic tuition rate," which offers significant savings over out-of-state tuition.

National Universities Degree Consortium (NUDC)

www.nudc.org

The National Universities Degree Consortium (NUDC) is a nation-wide collaborative of higher-education institutions, offering fully accredited courses and degree programs. Courses are delivered in flexible formats (including the Internet, audio and video, printed self-study materials, CD-ROM, and teleconferences). You can browse by school or degree program, or conduct a keyword search through all the course offerings.

SUNY Learning Network

http://sln.suny.edu/index.html

The State University of New York Learning Network of online pro-grams lists 100 degrees and certificate programs with over 4,300 individual courses. Unlike many other distance learning programs, courses listed here have specific start and end dates, which may be useful if you need help staying on track. Students enroll direct-ly in the institution offering the course or degree they're interested in. Tuition costs vary depending on campus, course level, and res-idency status.

Continuing Education, at a Distance

No degrees are available from the sites listed here, but if you want to try out a class or two for your own personal development, you're in the right place. Also, keep in mind that many other distance learning institutions allow students to take individual courses without enrolling in a degree program.

Barnes & Noble University

www.barnesandnobleuniversity.com

Online classes from a bookstore? Why not? Courses here are free, and they offer interaction with an instructor—often the author— and fellow students through online forums, anytime, anywhere. Barnes & Noble makes its money selling you required textbooks, but you are under no obligation to buy from them. Check out the free online moderated reading groups as well, offering the opportunity to discuss new and classic books.

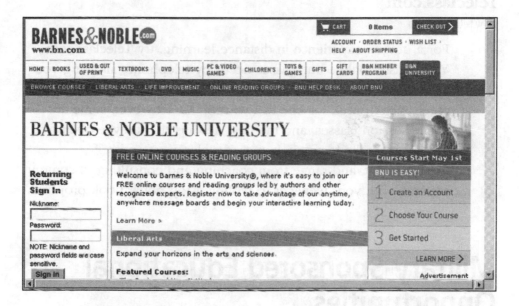

OnlineLearning.net

www.OnlineLearning.net

Busy teachers looking to meet professional development continuing-education requirements or lifelong learning objectives should investigate this specialized site's online options. Undergraduate and graduate degrees are not offered here, but you can earn transferable college credit for some of the online courses. You can also sign up with this site to create a personal start page and receive information on new courses and upcoming events.

Seminar Information Service

www.seminarinformation.com

If distance learning isn't your thing, the Seminar Information Service provides an easy way to search for more than 360,000 live, in-person seminars, classes, workshops, conferences, and corporate training events annually. Conduct a quick search by keyword, location, or date, or browse featured events each month. Most seminars provide the option to enroll online.

Teleclass.com

www.teleclass.com

For a unique experience in distance learning, try Teleclass.com. You register online but classes occur by telephone, allowing you to interact with an instructor and other students. Classes usually meet once a week for one or two months. However, some are single-session classes, and the best news is that they're often free. Topics generally focus on human development and self-improvement, and range from coaching and consulting to communicating with your teenager to writing a top-notch book proposal.

Military-Sponsored Educational Opportunities

The U.S. military recognizes the importance of education for all service members and sponsors both degree and continuing-education opportunities. A number of these are available online or through other distance learning methods so that active personnel can learn while serving their country, wherever they may be stationed. For information on joining or working for the military, see chapter 7.

Air University

www.au.af.mil/au/

For a comprehensive look at educational opportunities in the Air Force, visit Air University. Headquartered at Maxwell Air Force Base in Montgomery, Alabama, Air University is the Air Force's center for professional military education. It covers the full spectrum of education, from precommissioning to degree-granting and professional continuing education for officers, enlisted personnel, and civilians throughout their careers. We've provided more information on two programs—Air Force Institute for Advanced Distributed Learning and Community College of the Air Force—that provide distance learning.

Air Force Institute for Advanced Distributed Learning

www.maxwell.af.mil/au/afiadl/

The U.S. Air Force manages its own distance learning program for current personnel. Many courses are taught via satellite broadcasts or computer-assisted instruction. This site lists continuing education and for-credit offerings from a number of related organizations and Air Force divisions. Check out the Site Index for an overview of the comprehensive information contained here.

Community College of the Air Force

www.au.af.mil/au/ccaf/

The Community College of the Air Force is the only degree-granting institution of higher learning in the world dedicated to enlisted people. CCAF offers unique opportunities for active-duty Air National Guard, Air Force Reserve, and noncommissioned officers to earn a job-related, two-year undergraduate associate's degree in applied science. Thousands have done so. Since issuing its first degree in 1977, the college has awarded more than 275,000 associate's degrees in applied science. The site explains how to find out more about distance learning options through affiliated schools.

Credentialing Opportunities On-Line (COOL)

https://www.cool.army.mil/

> Start your planning here for a civilian career. COOL explains how
> Army soldiers can meet civilian certification and license require-
> ments related to their Military Occupational Specialties (MOSs).
> Identify civilian licensed occupations similar to your current mili-
> tary work, and learn how to fill the gaps between Army training
> and experience and civilian job credentials. Go to the COOL
> Overview for an easy-to-follow first-time visitors' guide to the site.

DANTES Distance Learning Programs

www.dantes.doded.mil

> Through agreements with a number of schools with existing dis-
> tance learning programs, DANTES provides distance learning
> opportunities to active service members in all branches of service
> who are in the process of earning their degrees, wherever they
> are stationed. Nondegree courses are also available for military
> personnel looking to improve their technical or other skills. Up to
> 75% of tuition costs can be reimbursed by DANTES or the appro-
> priate service branch upon successful completion of each course.
> For some distance learning inspiration, check out the success sto-
> ries in the monthly DANTES information bulletins posted online.

eArmyU.com

www.earmyu.com

eArmyU offers soldiers learning anytime, anywhere, in nearly 150 online degree programs through partnerships with more than 28 U.S. universities. First use the eligibility checklist (under "Resources") to see whether you qualify for the program. Then browse through the certificates and degrees that are offered, or search the catalog for specific courses in your area of interest. Subjects are broken into several "program communities." Mentors are available to advise students in their areas of study. Army personnel can earn credits, certificates, and degrees at a low cost or no cost while remaining on active duty. Each program enrollee receives a technology package for use in his or her studies, including a laptop preloaded with the appropriate software.

GI Bill

www.gibill.va.gov

Get the official word about the educational benefits offered by the GI Bill at this site. Important announcements are posted right on the front page of the site. Use the FAQ to find quick answers to the most frequently asked questions about the bill, and ask your own question via an online form if it is not answered there. You can also print copies of applications and other useful forms and find current news on rate changes and other program changes.

MarineNet

https://www.marinenet.usmc.mil/portal/

MarineNet is the gateway for online training for members of the Marine Corps. This site offers plenty of information to get you started, such as eligibility, computer requirements, and course descriptions, as well as self-education bonus promotion points and reserve retirement credits. Some courses offer college credit.

Navy College Program
https://www.navycollege.navy.mil/#

The mission of the Navy College Program is to help sailors earn college degrees by providing academic credit for Navy training, work experience, and off-duty education. Find out here about the Navy College Program for Afloat College Education, which offers undergraduate and graduate courses to sailors on sea duty assignments. The NCP Distance Learning Partnership Schools Program, also described here, helps sailors anywhere make maximum use of military professional training and experience to fulfill degree requirements and meet their educational goals.

Servicemembers Opportunity Colleges (SOC)
www.soc.aascu.org

This consortium of more than 1,800 colleges and universities allows U.S. military service members and their families to complete associate's and bachelor's degrees, no matter where they are stationed or how often they move. Courses are offered at Army, Navy, Marine Corps, and Coast Guard installations or via distance learning. Member colleges have agreed to accept each other's transfer credits. Start by reading "Why Participate in a SOC Program?" for basic information on SOC advantages and requirements. Then check out the links for each service branch for descriptions of specific programs, or download the current SOC Guide (in Adobe Acrobat format) for information on each participating institution and applicable policies.

U.S. Marine Corps College of Continuing Education

www.tecom.usmc.mil/cce/

If you're a Marine, learn about the many continuing-education opportunities open to you. In addition to the online learning network, MarineNet (described earlier), the College of Continuing Education offers training through learning resource centers and a video teletraining network. Also find out about the Command and Staff College and Expeditionary Warfare School Distance Education Seminar programs on officer professional military education. Experienced and diverse faculty members include active-duty and reserve Marines, government civilian employees, and contracted adjunct faculty.

CHAPTER **3**

Career Exploration Information

With all the career choices available to you, how do you choose? The Web sites in this chapter can help. We've organized them into categories to help you more easily find what you need. If you're just starting to think about a career, begin with the Web sites in the "Career Planning" section to get organized. The "Self-Assessment" sites provide a variety of tools for you to learn more about yourself and why some jobs may appeal to you more than others. The U.S. Department of Labor is an excellent source of a range of helpful information. We'll give you ideas of where to look. The section "State-Based Career Information" tells you how to find such an information system in your state.

And that's just for starters. The "Career Information Potpourri" section is a sampling of Web sites that provide a variety of career information aimed at a range of audiences, from high school students to older workers. We've included online resources for apprenticeship, job training, and salary information. We'll look at job benefits and tell you why being prepared for job loss is a sound career strategy.

Many job and resume banks, such as CareerBuilder and Monster, also feature articles and helpful information on career selection and exploration. These sites are grouped in chapter 4. Clearinghouses of career-related links (see chapter 5) are another great resource for identifying general and specific career information on the Web.

Career Planning

Career planning is simply a strategy to help you organize your career-selection efforts. There is no right or wrong way to decide which career to pursue. The problem is that so many people just don't know where to start. Here are some ideas.

Career Planning Steps

Every journey begins with a single step. These sites will get you going with practical suggestions and plenty of resources.

Career Development eManual
www.cdm.uwaterloo.ca

> This site is a gem and an excellent place to begin your personal career development process. The Career Development eManual from the staff at the University of Waterloo (Canada) Career Services Office walks you step-by-step through a time-tested planning process, complete with exercises, video interviews, and additional resources. The six steps are Self-Assessment, Research, Decision-Making (including Education), Networks & Contacts, Work, and Life/Work Planning. Packed with information without any distracting ads, this award-winning site provides a real public service.

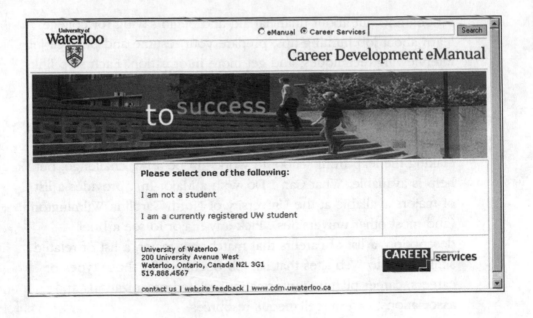

University of Waterloo
Waterloo

○ eManual ● Career Services [   ] [Search]

Career Development eManual

to success

Please select one of the following:

I am not a student

I am a currently registered UW student

University of Waterloo
200 University Avenue West
Waterloo, Ontario, Canada N2L 3G1
519.888.4567

CAREER services

contact us | website feedback | www.cdm.uwaterloo.ca

Career Planning Process

www.bgsu.edu/offices/sa/career/students/planning_process.html

The Career Planning Process from Bowling Green State University in Bowling Green, Ohio, outlines a career exploration model to help you gain competencies, make decisions, set goals, and take action. The steps are Self-Assessment, Academic/Career Options, Relevant/Practical Experience, Job Search/Graduate School Preparation, and Career Change. Although designed with the BGSU audience in mind, if you're looking for possible careers and can't figure out what to do next, this Web site can give you some clues.

Planning a Career

www.mapping-your-future.org/planning/

Although it's aimed at future college students, Planning a Career can be useful to anyone who wants information on choosing or changing a career. The ten straightforward steps to planning your career are develop a career plan, assess your skills and interests, research occupations, compare your skills and interests with the occupations you've selected, choose your career goal, select a school, find out about financial aid and begin saving for college, learn about job hunting tips, prepare your resume and practice job interviewing techniques, and get more information. Each step links to more information and tips.

What Can I Do With a Major In...

www.uncwil.edu/stuaff/career/Majors/index.htm

Making the leap from school to work can be a big challenge, but help is available. What Can I Do With a Major In... provides a list of majors available at the University of North Carolina Wilmington (and most other universities). Pick any major to see a brief description, a list of careers that match that major, a list of related skills, links to Web sites that list job openings for those types of careers, career planning information, related organizations and associations, and miscellaneous resources.

Self-Assessment

You might have noticed that the first step in the sites just discussed generally is self-assessment: the process of working to identify, understand, and express your skills, knowledge, abilities, interests, values, personality, motivations, passions, and anything else about you that might affect your career decisions. This makes sense. You need to figure out who you are and what you want before you can make an informed choice about your future (or next) career. But self-exploration can be a daunting task, so the Web sites in this section provide a variety of self-assessment tools to help you start this process, from validated tests administered by professionals to quizzes to writing or journaling exercises.

About Career Planning

http://careerplanning.about.com/od/selfassessment/

About.com scores with this section specifically on career planning. In addition to links to online career assessments, you can read up on how self-assessments fit into your career planning process, which is also described here in a four-step process. Know the difference between a values inventory and a personality inventory? You will after you visit this site and maybe even take an assessment or two.

AdvisorTeam

www.advisorteam.com/temperament_sorter/register.asp

Register for no fee and take the Keirsey Temperament Sorter II. This 70-question personality tool helps you discover your personality type, something that might be useful to know when making career decisions. Dr. David Keirsey's Temperament Theory sorts people into four temperament groups—artisans, guardians, rationals, and idealists—which are further sorted into 16 character types. You can read descriptions of the four temperament groups and their character types here as well.

The Big Five Personality Test

www.outofservice.com/bigfive/

UC Berkeley psychologist Frank J. Sulloway provides this 48-question test to measure "the five fundamental dimensions of personality." Its unique feature is that you are encouraged to answer each question both from your own perspective and as another person you know well. Your and the other person's percentile results (as compared to others who have taken this online test) are explained in five areas: Openness to Experience/Intellect, Conscientiousness, Extroversion, Agreeableness, and Neuroticism. You'll also find links to other personality sites on the Web that let you learn more about the Big Five approach and your results. This site is also available in German, Spanish, and Dutch.

The Career Key

www.careerkey.org

If you want to invest in a professional-quality career test, check out The Career Key. Based on Holland's Theory of Career Choice, The Career Key meets professional-level standards of reliability and validity. In other words, it measures what it sets out to measure, and it does so consistently. Take the assessment online for

$7.95 and read the articles on skills to better understand the theory. The Career Key is the work of Lawrence K. Jones, Ph.D., a professor emeritus from North Carolina State University and author of several career-related publications.

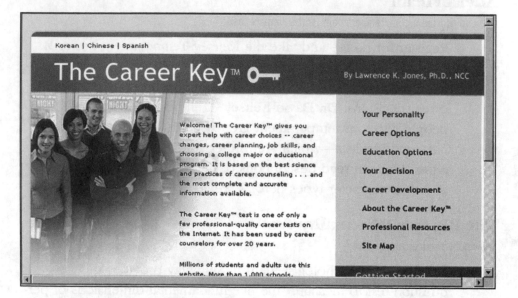

Enneagram Institute

www.enneagraminstitute.com

Learn about the Enneagram theory of nine personality types at this Web site by Don Richard Riso and Russ Hudson, two of the leading Enneagram teachers and developers. Take the sampler version of the Riso-Hudson Enneagram Type Indicator online to discover your type, or pay a fee for the full assessment and report. The site is a good source of other resources, including an active discussion board, books, and articles, for further exploration of this fascinating tool.

International Assessment Network: MAPP

www.assessment.com

Explore your career interests based on understanding what motivates you. MAPP stands for Motivational Appraisal of Personal Potential. Register for free to take a sample assessment intended to identify your motivations, interests, and talents. Your results and supporting material, including five job descriptions, are e-mailed to you. MAPP can produce a range of reports with additional information and assessments for a variety of fees. Sample reports and FAQs help you determine your individual needs.

Job Readiness Tests

www.businessworks.bc.ca/tests.htm

Take four online assessments of your personal management skills, your teamwork skills, your academic skills, and identifying your skills. Follow up with some suggestions on how to make the most of your results. These job readiness tests were developed by Business Works, a Canadian program helping job seekers and employers in British Columbia. The quick and simple online tests introduce you to the concept and language of self-assessments and may spur your interest in getting additional training in some areas.

O*NET Skills Search

http://online.onetcenter.org/skills/

Studies have shown that choosing a career based on skills you have and enjoy is a sound approach to career development. The O*NET Skills Search is designed to help you use your skill set to identify occupations for exploration. You start by selecting a set of skills from six broad groups of skills and creating your customized skill list. One click produces a list of occupations that match your skills, and another click on any of the occupations gives you a detailed report of that occupation. Report topics include tasks, knowledge, skills, abilities, work activities, work context, work styles, work values, related occupations, wages and employment, and more.

The Personality Page

www.personalitypage.com/

When you understand your personality, you may gain insight into what could make you happy in a career. Personality typing is based on the work of psychologist Carl Jung and, later, Isabel Briggs Meyers, who created the popular Myers-Briggs Type Indicator (MBTI). This site offers a 60-question personality questionnaire for a nominal fee that tells you which of 16 personality types you fit into. Alternatively, you can read about personality typing—and there's plenty here to read—and then categorize your own behavior. If you're still foggy on your own type, consider investing in having a professional administer and interpret the full MBTI for you. For more information, visit the Center for Applications of Psychological Type at www.capt.org.

Queendom.com Career Tests

www.queendom.com/tests/career

Are you suited for that IT job you're considering? Just for fun, find out by taking the IT Job Fit Test at Queendom.com. The site offers a large variety of tests (self-assessments, actually) in the areas of IQ, career, personality, and health. The number of tests available depends on whether you register for a fee or for free. The no-fee offerings are fairly generous as well as interesting, making a visit here worthwhile. Queendom.com's slogan is "Seriously entertaining."

Informational Interviewing

One of the best ways to learn more about the real-world aspects of a given career is by talking to people currently working in the field. This section shows you how.

Information Interviews (Florida State University)

www.career.fsu.edu/ccis/guides/infoint.html

If ads at other sites distract you, get the plain facts here. This site is a nice summary overview of the informational interviewing process, including why to do one, who you should contact, where you can find these people, and how you should prepare for your informational interview. You'll also find ideas on questions to ask, information on setting up the interview, pointers for handling the interview, and follow-up suggestions.

Informational Interview: About.com

http://jobsearch.about.com/cs/infointerviews/a/infointerview.htm

This section from the Job Searching directory in About.com provides the basics on informational interviewing—what to do before, during, and after. See a sample letter to send to set up an informational interview, review a list of questions to choose from, find out how to evaluate what you learned from the interview, and learn to write a good thank-you letter. You'll find plenty of links to additional reading and resources as well.

Quintessential Careers: Informational Interviewing Tutorial

www.quintcareers.com/informational_interviewing.html

This tutorial walks you through the informational interview process, from identifying people to interview to doing your homework beforehand to evaluating the information you receive. The information is laid out in an easy-to-follow outline. You'll also find a ton of sample questions to spark your thoughts on what you might ask your contact.

U.S. Department of Labor Career Information

An educated, well-trained workforce is a key element of a healthy economy. The U.S. Department of Labor (DOL) is the leading federal agency for employment-related programs and statistics. It shares its research and information with all job seekers through several comprehensive Web sites.

America's Career InfoNet

www.acinet.org/acinet/

America's Career InfoNet (ACINet) is part of the CareerOneStop suite of Web sites from the U.S. Department of Labor (see America's Job Bank and America's Service Locator in chapter 4). At this site, you'll find national, state, and local career information and labor market data using career reports, videos, a career resource library, and other innovative Web-based tools. Under Occupation Information, you can view occupation lists sorted by characteristics such as the fastest-growing or the most openings, or compare wages and trends. You can also build a profile of an occupation, choosing only the attributes you're most interested in. Industry Information lists the fastest-growing industries, those with the largest employment, and declining industries. State Information provides you with demographic, employment, and services data and links to state labor market information. ACINet also offers a series of interactive career tools for career, education, and business decisions.

Career Guide to Industries

www.bls.gov/oco/cg/

The Career Guide to Industries from the Bureau of Labor Statistics allows you to locate career information by industry. Just select a broad category from the links on the right, or choose the A–Z Index to search for a particular industry by name. Information on each includes the nature of the industry, working conditions, employment, occupations in the industry, training and advancement, outlook, earnings, and lists of organizations that can provide additional information. You might want to start with the "How Industries Differ" page for an overview of how understanding current industry conditions can help you find the job outlook and employment conditions for each. This is a companion guide to the *Occupational Outlook Handbook* (discussed in a moment).

Career Voyages

www.careervoyages.gov

Whether you're a student, career changer, parent of a young adult, or career advisor, you'll find helpful career information here. Career Voyages is a collaboration of the U.S. Department of Labor and U.S. Department of Education. It's designed to provide information on high-growth, high-demand occupations, along with the skills and education needed to attain those jobs. After you read an industry profile, you can find information on the hiring outlook and wages for in-demand careers and view career videos online. Or you can explore the "hot careers" by state, by those requiring a four-year degree, or by those requiring less than a four-year degree. The Career Compass helps you learn more about using your interests as a guide to career selection.

Certification Finder

www.acinet.org/acinet/certifications_new/cert_search_occupation.asp?id=14&nodeid=17

A certification is evidence that you have knowledge, experience, or skills in an occupation or profession, usually proven by successfully passing an exam and/or series of classes. This handy site from America's Career InfoNet lets you search for certifications by keyword, industry, or occupation. It lists certification and training providers alphabetically, with links to more information. Read the FAQs under Certification Finder Help for general information on certifications.

Licensed Occupations

www.careerinfonet.org/acinet/licensedoccupations/lois_state.asp

To work as a hunting and fishing guide in some states, you need a license. In others, you don't. How can you know? For starters, visit Licensed Occupations, part of America's CareerInfoNet Workforce Credentials Information Center. At this site you can search the database of licensed occupations by occupation, agency, or keyword, and locate the contact information for the state licensing agency. Get all the FAQs on licensed occupations in the Help section.

Occupational Outlook Handbook

www.bls.gov/oco/

Every two years, the Bureau of Labor Statistics produces the *Occupational Outlook Handbook*—the best-known and most comprehensive book on occupations. The online version contains the same information as the printed copy, without the illustrations. The best way to find details on a particular occupation is to search by job title. Each description provides extensive information on the nature of the work, working conditions, training and education needed, advancement potential, employment statistics, job outlook, earnings, links to related occupations, and sources of additional information. You can read online or download a printer-friendly version of each report. Don't have a specific title in mind? Browse by broad category (construction, professional, armed forces, and so on) to access a list of job titles, and then read about those that interest you.

O*NET OnLine

http://online.onetcenter.org

O*NET, the Occupational Information Network, contains comprehensive job descriptions, including tasks; required knowledge, skills, and abilities; work activities and content; wages and employment; and more. Search for occupations by keyword, classification code, or field, or browse by O*NET descriptors. You can also use the skills checklists to find occupations that use your existing skills. After you look up an occupation, you can read a brief description, request further details, or search for related jobs to get ideas on other directions in which to take your career. Because O*NET is intended to provide standardized information to job seekers and employers, each description uses the same format and includes the same types of information, making it easy to compare potential career choices.

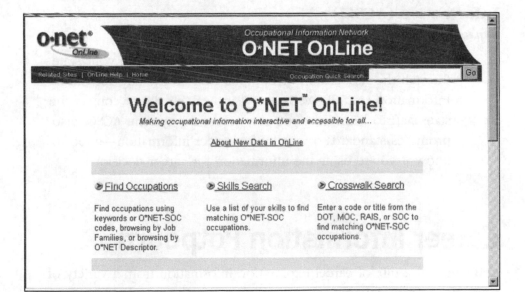

State-Based Career Information

Almost every state has a state-based career information system that contains searchable descriptions of occupations, programs of study, state and national colleges, private vocational schools, financial aid, scholarships, and more. The term "state-based" means that these state programs typically update the information annually and include salary ranges and hiring outlooks for occupations within that state. Because this data can and does vary in different areas of the country, the information in state-based systems is more detailed than similar nationwide data.

State-based career information system software programs are found in elementary schools, middle schools, and high schools; colleges and universities; job-training program sites; state workforce development sites; libraries; and other agencies serving the public.

Association of Computer-Based Systems for Career Information (ACSCI)

www.acsci.org/

> Link to the state-based career information system in your state through the Association of Computer-Based Systems for Career Information (ACSCI) Web site. Visit the Web site or contact the state staff to learn how you can access the system. ACSCI also promotes standards of quality for career information—good to know if you're using the information for career decisions.

Career Information Potpourri

You can find a mix of career exploration information from a variety of sources: professional associations, online newspapers and magazines, publishers, agencies, and more.

AARP: Careers

www.aarp.org/money/careers

> Workers over the age of 45 make up 37 percent of the workforce, according to the U.S. Census Bureau. And the percentage of employees over the age of 65 is higher now than in the past 20

years. With over 35 million members, AARP is the leading non-profit, nonpartisan membership organization for Americans age 50 and over. This section of the AARP Web site covers choosing a career, job loss help, self-employment, and workplace flexibility with articles geared toward its members. In addition to basic career and job search information, find out about alternative work arrangements, discover clues that an employer welcomes older workers, learn about age-neutral employment practices, and get informed on how job accommodations can let you continue working even if you have a health condition or disability.

American Society of Association Executives (ASAE)

www.asaecenter.org

ASAE has a nice collection of information on careers in association management. Even better, it has links or contact information on all kinds of professional organizations. Go to the Directories link and choose Gateway to Associations to find a database that can be searched by name, location, or category/keyword. Associations are good sources of career information because they are concerned with the growth and quality of their profession, and they typically provide member services, conferences, and education programs. In addition, some publish booklets or pamphlets for those considering the profession.

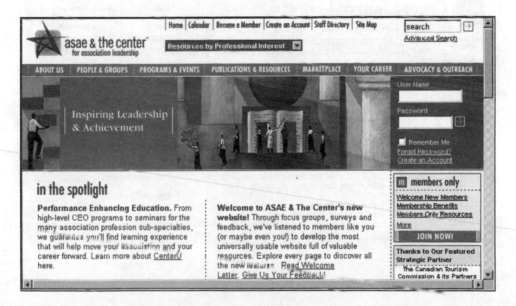

Barbara Sher

www.barbarasher.com

The outstanding feature on best-selling career author Barbara Sher's Web site are the extensive, active forums on a variety of subjects. Topics range from success stories to idea parties. Your questions can be answered by fellow members or by Sher herself. You'll also find ideas on starting your own "Success Team" with friends or finding a certified team leader near you. (Members of Success Teams support each other in achieving their dreams.)

CareerJournal.com

www.careerjournal.com

CareerJournal.com is loaded with information on all aspects of careers, but this should come as no surprise, since it's from the *Wall Street Journal*. Salary information, job hunting advice, human resources issues, executive recruiting, college information—it's all here. Find daily feature career articles, search the database of free and low-cost events, join discussion boards, and read special reports. You can also add your resume to the database or sign up for customized e-mail job listings. Click the site map link to access all articles and resources by subject area.

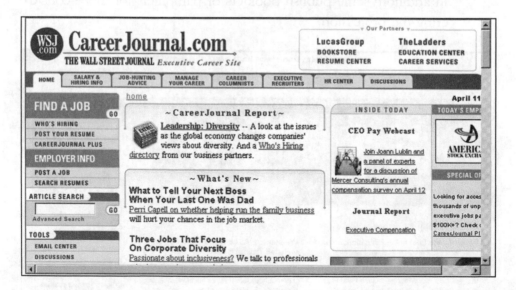

Careers in Business

www.careers-in-business.com

If you mean business about having a business career, check out this site. Careers in Business profiles careers in accounting, consulting, finance, marketing, and nonprofit management, providing information on skills, job options, salaries, trends, top firms, and recommended books on the subject. Scroll down the main page for a list of links to other recommended career sites.

getcareerskills.com

www.acteonline.org/career/skills

High school students can learn about technical careers and education at getcareerskills.com, a service of the Association for Career and Technical Education (ACTE). Click an industry category and a table pops up listing occupations, average annual earnings, required education, and follow-up contact Web sites. The ACTE site also has information and handy links to career and technical student organizations, such as Business Professionals of America, Technology Students Association, and Distributive Education Clubs of America, and other resources as well.

JIST Publishing

www.jist.com

JIST Publishing is your source for the best career, job search, business, and self-help books, videos, and software available today. This Web site delivers free career resources and weekly career-related tips, such as Mike Farr's online Get a Job workshop and Best Jobs lists. Visit the site, browse the catalog online, request a free print catalog, and see for yourself. You can sign up for free e-mail newsletters, including "The Jist of It," which offers practical, self-directed information and articles that you can use in your work.

Job Accommodation Network (JAN)

www.jan.wvu.edu

The purpose of JAN is to increase the employability of persons with disabilities. Through funding from the U.S. Department of Labor Office of Disability Employment Policy, JAN consultants work with people with disabilities and employers to create accommodation solutions that benefit and contribute to the hiring, retention, and promotion of this special-needs group. Services include toll-free consultations on employment, self-employment, and small-business options for persons with disabilities. The Web site contains over 300 disability-specific publications, resources for purchasing accommodation equipment, and links to thousands of local, regional, national, public, and private resource organizations.

JobProfiles.org

www.jobprofiles.org

For firsthand accounts from successful individuals in a variety of careers, visit JobProfiles.com. The profiles consist of questionnaires asking about the rewards, stress, basic skills, and challenges of jobs, as well as advice on entering the field. Organized by field of work, the profiles range from jobs in agriculture and nature to government and retail sales. Browse by category or search for profiles by keyword. Although one person's perspective on a job or career may not be shared by everyone in that line of work, JobProfiles.com does provide a unique, insider's view of real-world work. This is recommended reading before you do informational interviews (as described earlier in this chapter).

MyCareerBlast.com

www.mycareerblast.com

If you're on the verge of making the transition from school to the working world, this site is for you. At MyCareerBlast.com, you can get advice about choosing a college major or minor, uncover summer jobs and internships, get help with grad school decisions, read articles about achieving success on your first job, and find resources about freelancing or starting a business. All this is in addition to searching for a job and posting your resume.

Pam Pohly's Net Guide
www.pohly.com/index.html

> If you're interested in a career in healthcare, you will want to bookmark this site. Pam Pohly Associates is a national management consulting firm with exclusive specialization in healthcare. Here you will find loads of resources covering all aspects of the business of healthcare, from personnel management to a glossary of managed-healthcare terms. This site also has links and contact information for state and regional hospital associations, healthcare and medical professional associations, healthcare recruiters, healthcare companies and hospitals, professional journals, and much more.

Apprenticeships and Job Training

Apprenticeship and job training programs mix classroom work with on-the-job training and provide entry into high-skill, rewarding professions. For more information on these and other job training programs (in the U.S.), contact the workforce development office in your state (see chapter 4).

Canadian Apprenticeship Forum
www.caf-fca.org/english/index.asp

> The Canadian Apprenticeship Forum (CAF-FCA) is a not-for-profit organization that promotes and supports the apprenticeship training and education systems in Canada. In Canada, each province or territory is responsible for setting the rules and regulations for apprenticeship training, and a special "Red Seal" endorsement permits skilled tradespeople to work anywhere in Canada. Here you'll find links to each provincial/territorial governmental apprenticeship Web site, as well as FAQs for both apprentices and employers. This site is available in both English and French.

Job Corps

http://jobcorps.doleta.gov

Job Corps is a no-cost education and vocational training program administered by the U.S. Department of Labor that helps young people ages 16 to 24 get a better job, make more money, and take control of their lives. Find out about the program, eligibility requirements, and interview process online, download the Job Corps information brochure, and then call the 800 number to get your questions answered and be referred to a local admissions counselor. If you've already gone through the program, you can join the National Job Corps Alumni Association.

Registered Apprenticeship

www.doleta.gov/atels_bat/

This site from the U.S. Department of Labor serves both individuals looking for apprenticeships and employers seeking to set up apprenticeship programs. This is your source of general information about apprenticeship programs in the U.S. as well as links to places to find a program. Apprenticeships teach a trade through a combination of on-the-job training and related instruction. They can be one of the best ways to learn the ins and outs of a particular occupation.

Salary Information

Use the sites in this section to learn the average pay rates in your chosen field, get tips on salary negotiation, and find cost-of-living information for different parts of the country.

JobStar: Salary Info Index

http://jobstar.org/tools/salary/

Although this site also has career guides and resume information, JobStar is best known for its salary information. It's tempting to jump directly to JobStar's more than 300 links to general and profession-specific salary surveys, but take some time to explore salary-negotiation strategies and test your own salary IQ first. Information on print resources you might want to check out is also included.

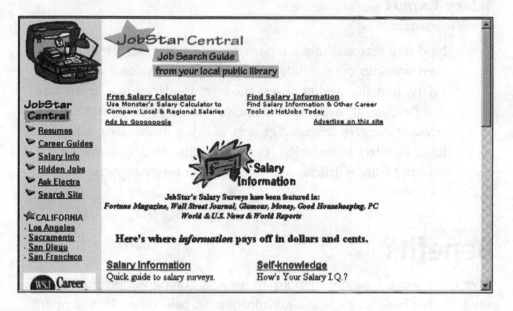

Quintessential Careers: Salary-Negotiation Tools

www.quintcareers.com/salary_negotiation.html

Don't get intimidated at the thought of negotiating a salary—get educated! Quintessential Careers offers a salary-negotiation tutorial for starters and a salary negotiation, compensation, and job offer quiz to test your skills. Learn how to write a counterproposal to bump up that job offer, see suggestions for dealing with salary history requests, and learn the basic do's and don'ts of salary negotiations. Anyone can negotiate a salary. Some time invested here can pay big dividends down the road of your career.

The Salary Calculator

www.homefair.com/calc/salcalc.html

Thinking about relocating for a job? Compare the cost of living among hundreds of U.S. and international cities with this handy salary calculator from HomeFair.com. Just enter your salary and current location, and then select another city to find out what you'll need to make there to sustain the same standard of living. While here, check out other relocation tools as well.

Salary Expert
www.salaryexpert.com

Find free regional salary reports by selecting your job title and then your zip code or city. Reports list the position's average salary, benefits, and bonuses; show how salaries in a given area compare to the national average; provide a brief description of the occupation; give the average cost of living in the area; and list links to salary information for related jobs. Also available here are selected feature articles and international salary reports.

Benefits

Most of us work for more than a paycheck. A compensation package ideally includes benefits such as health insurance, paid time off, retirement, savings programs, and a variety of other offerings. Benefits vary widely from organization to organization, and employers use a good benefits package as a hiring incentive. Understanding what benefits are, and appreciating their value to you, can help you identify employers you'd like to work for.

Office of Personnel Management: Employment and Benefits
www.opm.gov/Employment_and_Benefits/index.asp

The U.S. federal government has long been well regarded for its employment benefits. This site explains them, providing helpful general information even if you don't intend to work for the government. Familiarize yourself with such terms as fee-for-service, preferred provider organization, health maintenance organization, flexible spending accounts, and long-term care insurance to become a better-informed job seeker.

Job Loss Strategies

Layoffs occur for a host of reasons: automation, bankruptcy, a business ownership change, contracts completed or canceled, foreign competition, natural disasters, and more. When you hear about them in the news, it's merely news. When you're caught in the middle, it's your livelihood. But, as these sites point out, this doesn't have to be cause for despair.

After a Job Loss

www.careerjournal.com/jobhunting/jobloss

> This section of CareerJournal.com from the *Wall Street Journal* presents pages of articles on all aspects of dealing with a job loss. Topics range from establishing job search support systems to regaining your confidence after a major setback and helping your family members cope with the change too. Inspiring and informative reading at a time when you need it most.

Job Loss

www.nefe.org/fple/joblosspage1.html

> Losing your job unexpectedly can be one of the most traumatic experiences of your life. And unfortunately, with the ever-changing job market and economic conditions, this can be a real possibility over the course of your career. At this site, the National Endowment for Financial Education presents an online brochure to help you weather the storm and see you through to better times. It contains practical advice, suggestions for action steps, and a list of print resources.

What To Do If You're Being Laid Off

www.investsafe.com/development/
advice.html?OVRAW=%22job%20loss%22&OVKEY=job%20loss&OVMTC=standard

> The answer: Go to this Web site and read through the 39 tips for coping with job loss. A little preparation and smart thinking can go a long way toward easing the pain of job loss and speeding up the regrouping and transition process. It's good to know where to look for practical advice if and when you need it.

CHAPTER 4

Finding and Applying for Job Openings

One thing is for sure—the Internet has no shortage of job information, nor will it in the future. In the early days of the Internet, employment professionals and recruiters saw the Internet's tremendous potential, with its ability to reach millions of people, and they jumped on with enthusiasm. Over the years, three trends have emerged: General job bank sites have gotten bigger and have become more sophisticated with search capabilities, the number of specialty job banks is growing, and almost all of the sites now want you to register, either for free or for a fee.

Typical features on these sites include the ability to search and apply for jobs, post your resume for employers to view, and be notified of openings that match criteria you establish. Job banks usually charge employers and recruiters to post positions. Most sites allow you to search their listings but require you to register before you can apply.

Registering means different things on different sites. Some sites only ask you for a valid e-mail address and password. Others request more extensive information, using it to compile a demographic profile of their customers and to elicit more business from employers and advertisers. The sites or their affiliates might also send you advertising. Look for a privacy policy regarding the use of your personal information, which should also clarify your opt-out options. If privacy is an issue for you, use only a job bank whose policies you understand and accept.

Speaking of advertising, be forewarned—the noncommercial job bank has become something of a rarity. A pop-up blocker can eliminate the most annoying ads. If action ads distract you, you can probably find a site without them. In addition to visual ads, several sites promote fee-based job search services such as resume writing and job coaching.

Consider limiting the number of job bank sites you use. With all you have to choose from, you can be selective. Try searching for the same job or job type in several job banks, and evaluate the results. How current is the information? Are posting dates listed? Do the positions come directly from employers, or are they from recruiters? Does the site provide good contact information on the companies, with links to their Web sites? After thoroughly evaluating several sites, you will decide on your favorites. Happy job hunting!

Government Sources of Job Information

Let's start with the Internet resources that are funded with your tax dollars. Both state and federal governments sponsor employment-related Internet sites that can link you to a number of job listings. (For information on jobs with the government itself, see the listings in the section "Other Specialized Job Banks" later in this chapter.)

U.S. Department of Labor

America's Job Bank
www.ajb.dni.us

The flagship component of the Department of Labor's (DOL's) CareerOneStop toolkit, America's Job Bank (AJB) offers a database of nearly two million job listings, with thousands more added daily. The nationwide listings in AJB represent all kinds of work, most of it full-time, private-sector employment. AJB is one of the few job banks that doesn't charge either job seekers or employers that list job vacancies, but both must register to fully access the site. Services for job seekers include resume posting and creation, an automated job scout, and lots of links to other resources. These are organized by topic, including relocation assistance, skills center, training and education, career tools, and more. Search by job category, title, keyword, degree or certificate required, military-only, or posting number. You can even limit searches to within 50 miles of your zip code. Unfortunately, this site will be phased out by July 2007.

America's Service Locator

www.servicelocator.org

Find the local workforce services you need through America's Service Locator. One-stop career centers, located in every state, provide convenient services to workers and employers, such as information on job training programs, unemployment insurance, education opportunities, career services, and more. Search for the center nearest you by city or zip code and get the address, complete with driving instructions and a map. For handy, up-to-date links to your state's workforce-related Web sites, see the state Web directory. America's Service Locator is part of the DOL's

CareerOneStop toolkit (see America's Job Bank, just described, and America's Career InfoNet, described in chapter 3).

General Job Banks

General Internet job banks draw from different sources and present their job postings in different ways. Visit several to see what we mean and find the ones you like the best.

BestJobsUSA.com

www.bestjobsusa.com

BestJobsUSA monitors over 300 major newspapers' employment sections each day. Try the state site selection option, which includes a separate jobs page focused on each U.S. state. On each of these pages, you can conduct a job search in only that state and find local articles and information. Registered job seekers have the option of posting and managing their resumes online, with an optional masking option to hide personal and contact information. Also check out the virtual career fairs, corporate profiles, and various lists of top employers.

CareerBuilder.com

www.careerbuilder.com

Search the classifieds of over 130 newspapers at this one handy site. CareerBuilder.com lets you sort by keyword, city, state, field of interest, company, industry, or job type. You can set up a Personal Search Agent to have matching jobs e-mailed to your inbox. You also can post your resume online (at your choice of three different privacy levels). Free registration entitles you to additional services such as job search management and resume posting tools.

LinkedIn

www.linkedin.com

> Discover the power of networking. When you join LinkedIn, you
> create a profile that summarizes your professional accomplish-
> ments. Through the LinkedIn network, you can find potential
> clients, service providers, subject experts, and partners who come
> recommended and discover inside connections that can help you
> land jobs. Job openings include not only the name of the person
> posting the position but also anyone else you and your contacts
> may connect to in the organization. Additional services come with
> paid membership.

Monster

www.monster.com

Monster, possibly the best-known career site on the Internet, contains all the features you'd expect from a major job and resume bank. Get tips on getting the most out of the site by visiting the Career Advice section. Your options here include registering to post your resume, having jobs e-mailed to you, signing up for e-mail newsletters, searching more than one million monthly job postings, and applying online using your posted resume. You'll also find advice, articles, discussion boards, and tools in an extensive online career center. Monster also offers additional services for a fee, such as resume writing assistance and career coaching.

NationJob

www.nationjob.com

Search for jobs or sign up to have P.J. Scout do it for you. Just tell him exactly what you want, and whenever he finds a job opening of interest to you, he will e-mail you a detailed job description, including "how to apply" information. All you need is an e-mail address. No e-mail address? No problem. P.J. can steer you to free, Web-based e-mail providers. Read job seeker success stories, browse company profiles, and even subscribe for free to trade magazines.

NowHiring.com

www.nowhiring.com

NowHiring.com offers personalized search agents, automatic matching of jobs against your resume, and expert advice. Start with the simple and straightforward User Guide for help in getting the most out of the site. Browse through hundreds of company profiles, or do an advanced search that allows you to select keywords, locations, job categories, salary level—even specific newspapers. Registering (for no charge) allows you to save your resumes and cover letters online, be notified when new postings match your search requirements, and take online job interviews.

Vault.com

www.vault.com

Vault is known for its insider information on more than 3,000 companies and 70 industries. Vault's Electronic Watercooler (under "Community") is the Internet's first collection of company-specific message boards for employees, where anyone can network, ask for job advice, or learn what it's like to work for a certain company. A Day in the Life features profiles of working professionals. Other features include sample cover letters, resumes, and interview questions. More information is available for a fee. All of this is in addition to the job bank itself and resume posting and matching services.

Yahoo! HotJobs

http://hotjobs.yahoo.com

> Use the advanced search feature at HotJobs to refine your results list. Under Advanced Job Search, you can search by keyword, up to three job categories or two locations, level of experience, and minimum salary. You can also screen out jobs posted by staffing firms if you want to deal directly with employers rather than applying through agencies. Your search results come in three flavors: sponsor companies, which pay for premium placement in search results; featured results, from organizations that have paid for the listings; and job listings that have been collected from across the Web. You must log in to post a resume or save your search results, but if you already have a Yahoo! e-mail account, it's your same username and password.

Job Banks for Recent or Soon-to-Be College Graduates

The sites in this section represent a large variety of work opportunities and career advice targeted at college students and recent graduates. If you're new to the workforce, you might find your ideal entry-level job here more easily than you would at a larger job bank.

AfterCollege

www.aftercollege.com

> Search among the more than 150,000 entry-level jobs from over 25,000 employers. AfterCollege also has listings of internships, guides for working abroad, and job channels to help you focus your search. And don't forget the resume-posting service, which converts any resume written in most common word processing programs.

The Black Collegian Online

www.black-collegian.com

> This award-winning site is the cyberspace partner of *The Black Collegian* magazine, serving the career and self-development interests of African-American college students since 1970. This site has plenty of career planning and job search information, as well as lifestyle/entertainment features and college life news. Post your resume or review job openings with equal-opportunity employers. Also check out the Diversity Registry for information on employers that actively recruit college students, particularly minorities, for entry-level jobs.

CollegeGrad.com

www.collegegrad.com

> CollegeGrad.com is devoted to entry-level job information. It contains extensive resources for new graduates seeking to enter the job market. Sections include career planning, resumes, cover letters, employer research, job postings, interviewing, salaries, and your new job. Also take a look at top entry-level employers, and check out the online career forum for employment advice. The job search section is broken into entry-level, internships, and experience required categories, helping you zero in on your best opportunities.

CollegeRecruiter.com

www.collegerecruiter.com

> Conduct a traditional job search, or browse openings by career channel. Free membership allows you to post your resume and have job notices e-mailed to you. In addition, CollegeRecruiter.com features a nice collection of industry information, including hiring prospects, the most common personality types for specific occupations, and career videos. Free industry magazines, blogs, podcasts, and even a couple of games are here as well.

InternJobs.com

www.internjobs.com

InternJobs.com is a global database of internships for students, recent graduates, and career changers. Search by location, keyword, or top jobs. Postings are generous in the information they provide. They include complete information on the hiring organization, including a link to the company Web site for further investigation.

JobWeb

www.jobweb.com

You won't find specific job openings at JobWeb, but you will find an extensive, searchable database of employers looking for career-minded graduates. Sponsored by the National Association of Colleges and Employers, JobWeb's primary audience is recent or soon-to-be college graduates. Other sections include resume and interview advice and a large library of career-related articles and career-planning information.

MonsterTRAK

www.monstertrak.monster.com

If your school is registered with MonsterTRAK, a division of Monster, many services are at your fingertips here, including searching for that first job or internship. Get career advice and networking opportunities from alums at your own school, research companies, participate in message boards and chats, find resume advice, and browse an online career fair. You'll also find career-related articles and tools, as well as a handy major-to-career converter tool to help you answer that all-important question: "What can I do with my major?"

Saludos.com

www.saludos.com

Saludos.com specializes in joining Hispanic bilingual professionals with companies looking for diversity in the workplace. Services for job seekers include listings of entry-level jobs and internships, a resume posting service, guides to researching specific fields, and additional career links. You'll also find online articles from *Saludos Hispanos* magazine.

TrueCareers

www.truecareers.com

TrueCareers is sponsored by Sallie Mae, the leading provider of education loans. It is designed to help borrowers and other college-educated candidates find higher-paying or more satisfying jobs. In addition to the job search and resume posting features, TrueCareers has company profiles, career articles, a diversity center, and an "ask the expert" discussion feature.

Other Specialized Job Banks

Specialized job banks aimed at specific groups or targeted to a particular field are one of the best ways to zero in on appropriate listings and cut through the clutter of crowded general databases. This section contains a sampling of the resources available. You can find more by browsing the clearinghouses described in the next chapter or by conducting an online search, as explained in the Introduction to this book.

911hotjobs.com

http://911hotjobs.com

If careers in law enforcement or firefighting sound exciting, call on 911hotjobs.com. Search free job listings, or sign up as a paid member to search jobs from 911hotjobs.com together with those from other law enforcement Web sites. The membership fee is charged monthly to your credit card, and you can cancel at any time. You can also order law enforcement employment and examination preparation books, sign up for a newsletter that notifies you when new positions are posted, or, for a fee, take online practice tests.

Cool Works

www.coolworks.com

If ski resorts, dude ranches, national parks, and cruises sound like fun places to work, get the scoop at the specialized job bank that is Cool Works. If you detect a note of enthusiasm for the types of jobs posted here, it may be because Cool Works is within shouting distance of Yellowstone National Park. Find the right adventure—internships, volunteer opportunities, guide jobs, conservation corps, and more—in addition to seasonal jobs. Visit the Get Started page under Job Seekers for helpful instructions on using the site. The Cool Works motto is "Thousands of jobs in great places."

dice.com

www.dice.com

Dice.com specializes in jobs for information technology (IT) professionals. Given the nature of the IT marketplace, a number of listings here are for contract positions rather than permanent opportunities. You can search the jobs by keyword, location, area code, type, and company. You can limit your search to telecommuting only or by the amount of travel required. You can also create a personalized account to have your profile available to employers (publicly or confidentially), create an online resume, and use personal search agents.

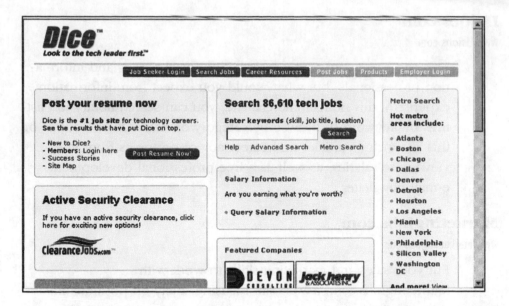

govtjobs.com

www.govtjobs.com

Govtjobs.com matches applicants with state, county, and local government job listings. Check out the posted job opportunities organized by job categories. Govtjobs.com also has links to almost 150 national associations and federal agencies, as well as state-by-state resource information where you can go exploring for job opportunities. Better yet, no registration or membership is required to access the information.

LatPro

www.latpro.com

LatPro claims to be the largest diversity employment Web site in the U.S. and the leading source for Spanish/English and Portuguese/English bilinguals throughout the Americas. A list of testimonials speaks highly of the site, which includes job search and resume posting features, career-related articles, e-mail newsletters, extensive information on immigration, and more. This site is available in English, Spanish, and Portuguese.

Lisjobs.com

www.lisjobs.com

This site has lots of career information for librarians and information professionals, but what would you expect from information experts? At this noncommercial site, you can search library job listings by keyword or browse by category or state. Other features on this site include articles and career advice on topics from interviewing to salaries, as well as a free professional development e-mail newsletter.

MarketingJobs.com

www.marketingjobs.com

Put your sales and marketing skills to work with MarketingJobs.com, a Web site focusing solely on positions in sales, marketing, and advertising. Search by keyword, job function, or state, or register and create an anonymous career profile and let employers find you. There aren't a lot of extras here, but if marketing is your career of choice, it's well worth the visit.

National Teacher Recruitment Clearinghouse

www.recruitingteachers.org

Find out about the teaching profession and the requirements for becoming a teacher, get tips on finding a teaching position, and learn about licensing in each state. The biggest plus of this site is its nationwide job bank portal. It's a metasearch clearinghouse that lets you find teacher job banks specific to your location and that lets you look for state, nationwide, or international job banks. But you have to register first. You can also locate the Department of Education in your state.

SeniorJobBank

www.seniorjobbank.org

The workers of tomorrow are here today, and they have a ton of experience. SeniorJobBank is aimed at the over-50 crowd, and anyone who is demographic-savvy knows that there are a lot of folks in this age group. In addition to industry, job category, and location, the search tool lets you choose the type of employment, ranging from short-term contract to full-time. Create up to three resumes with your free account with the option of allowing potential employers to view it, or have the personal job agent notify you of openings.

SummerJobs.com

www.summerjobs.com

Need to find summer or seasonal employment between semesters? SummerJobs.com is the place to start. Most of these ads come from camps, resorts, amusement parks, and other places that need seasonal help. You can also view employer profiles and links to their Web sites to find out about your potential summer employer. SummerJobs.com is part of the AboutJobs.com network.

USAJOBS

www.usajobs.opm.gov

USAJOBS is the official site of the U.S. Office of Personnel Management. It's a good place to go for information on working for the federal government. The powerful search feature lets you sort current job openings by keyword, location, job category, salary range, federal pay grade, job series, agency, and more. To get started, you can view online job search and resume tutorials or download handy reference guides. The Career Interests Center helps you assess your skills and interests and match them to potential federal opportunities. Additional information spells out everything you need to know and do to apply for a job, right down to completing the online resume.

Regional Job Sites

If you're less than geographically mobile, or if you're interested in employment in a particular region, you might want to investigate job banks specializing in positions and career advice for specific large cities, states, or regions. This section contains a few examples.

FloridaJobs.com

www.floridajobs.com

As the name suggests, FloridaJobs.com specializes in connecting Florida jobs and job seekers. After you register (for no cost), you can post a resume, with privacy options for how your information is used. You'll also find some tips and guidelines for taking full advantage of the site's offerings.

LocalJobBoard.com

www.localjobboard.com

If you're unwilling or unable to relocate to find a job, try LocalJobBoard.com. All the jobs posted here are categorized by city, state, and industry, and some 3,925 cities have job postings. It's searchable, of course, and, as with most job banks, you can post your resume and create a job alert with a free membership. A nice extra is the local information—economy, employment, real estate, recreation, schools, and sports.

TriStateJobs.com

www.tristatejobs.com

If you live in the Northeast, you might want to visit TriStateJobs.com for thousands of listings in New York, New Jersey, Connecticut, and Pennsylvania. You can search, post your resume, and sign up for e-mail notification of jobs matching your specifications. You also can check out information on local career fairs and find links to additional career sites and resources.

Tucson.Jobing.com

http://tucson.jobing.com/

One of several local job banks run by Jobing.com, this site allows you to search online for job openings in greater Tucson or in five other areas of the city. With a free online account, you can build up to ten resumes and cover letters; make your resume searchable, confidential, or hide it from individual employers; store and view the jobs for which you've applied; and create jobs–by–e-mail agents to notify you of openings.

Wisconsin Employment Connection

www.dwd.state.wi.us/dws/wec/tourism/regionalwebs.htm

> Find your dream job in Wisconsin through the Wisconsin Employment Connection. Pick a region of the state and link up with the local job resources, such as area newspapers, state job center offices, public libraries, universities, and more, many of which have their own job listings.

Canadian Job Information

This section contains leads to jobs in Canada. For information on jobs in other countries, check the career clearinghouses listed in chapter 5, as well as Monster and other job banks described in this chapter, several of which provide international listings or affiliate sites. Be aware, however, that many of these postings may be only for resident citizens.

Human Resources and Skills Development Canada: Job Bank

www.jobbank.gc.ca

> On any given day, Job Bank contains about 40,000 job postings across Canada, including a special section for student jobs. Pick your desired province, and then specify a job title or search by keyword to retrieve postings. You'll find a link to the Canadian Citizenship and Immigration Office for information on receiving an employment authorization if you are not a citizen or permanent resident. Job Bank also provides a number of links to other sites that are useful to Canadian job seekers. This site also is available in French.

Jobboom

www.jobboom.com

> At Jobboom, you can search for a specific job or an employer in Canada, subscribe to the weekly *Boomerang* e-zine, or view the top 100 Internet sites for learning and employment in Canada.

Registration is required to view some information and to apply for openings, but it's free, simple, and confidential. This site also is available in French.

Workopolis.com

www.workopolis.com

Search through more than 40,000 jobs in Canada, subscribe to a weekly JobMail newsletter, or take a tutorial in resume writing, networking, interviewing, or salary negotiation. Try the RSS (Really Simple Syndication) feature to have openings for job titles you select delivered to you in real time. Another handy feature is a direct link to the employer Web site for each posting for background research. Workopolis is a partnership of three Canadian media companies and appears in both English and French.

Getting the Job

You've honed your Web job searching skills. Now, what's the best way to go about applying for, and landing, the perfect job? Check out the sites in the following sections for some tips that take you the rest of the way.

Certify Yourself

This is essentially a fee-based service, but a unique and intriguing one that may start a trend.

CareerCertify.com

http://careercertify.com

If your career field does not have its own professional certification process, check out this site. The CareerCertify Skill Certification Center lets you confirm that you have the skills for the job you want. Career areas include accounting and financial, administrative and clerical, information technology, healthcare, IT management, engineering, sales and marketing, and managerial. Test your skills for free, and pay only to certify your skills. If you discover you need to brush up on your skills through the testing process, this site provides targeted learning recommendations. You can also pay to have CareerCertify.com do a background check on you. Why? Because a certified, prescreened job seeker saves the employer valuable time and money, giving that person an advantage over the competition.

Resumes and Cover Letters

Read about electronic resumes in the Introduction to this book, and then extend your resume creation and cover letter skills by browsing the Web sites described here.

CareerJournal.com: Resumes/Cover Letters

www.careerjournal.com/jobhunting/resumes

Get the latest scoop on resumes from the experts at the *Wall Street Journal's* CareerJournal.com. After you understand resume writing basics, visit this site for more detailed information, such as how-to articles on avoiding resume bloopers, creating a resume for foreign markets, patterning your resume on leaders in your field, and much more.

eResumes & Resume Writing Services

www.eresumes.com

Resume help, tips, formats, examples, cover letters, online resumes, professional resumes, free resumes, e-resumes—you name it, this site has it. For a new twist on resumes, check out this site's electronic employability (E2) portfolio. Read about the process and concept, and then see some real examples.

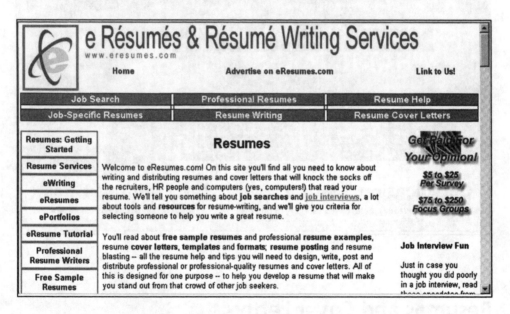

JobStar: Resumes & Cover Letters

http://jobstar.org/tools/resume/

JobStar's section on resumes and cover letters is categorized into several useful topics: What Is a Resume?, What Is the Right Resume for Me?, Resume Samples, Selected Resume Resources on the Web, Resume Tips, Electronic Resume Banks, About Cover Letters, and Sample Cover Letters. If you don't know the difference between a chronological resume and a functional one, you've come to the right place.

The Riley Guide: Resumes & Cover Letters
www.rileyguide.com/eresume.html

> No ads or action here—just a down-to-business site with some top-notch information. This particular page in the well-known Riley Guide (see chapter 5) thoroughly explains what you should know before posting a resume online. It has plenty of pointers on content and formatting, choosing a job site, and staying cyber-safe. Links here take you to more job search information in the Riley Guide.

Vault.com: Sample Cover Letters
www.vault.com/nr/ht_list.jsp?ht_type=9

> On this page, Vault.com (described earlier) has a nice collection of cover letters for a range of positions, from amusement park employee to electrical engineer to investment banker to disaster relief worker. Visit other sites to learn about cover letter writing, and then see some cover letters in action.

Career Portfolios

A career portfolio is a collection of documents supporting your career aspirations, such as a resume, letters of recommendation, awards, certificates, articles, and so on. The Web sites in this section tell you what a career portfolio is, how it differs from a resume, how to create your own, and how to use it effectively.

Creating Your Portfolio
http://www2.biz.colostate.edu/career/portfolio.htm

> At this site, the Colorado State University College of Business spells out a simple process for assembling your own career portfolio. Learn what to include and what to leave out. Read some tips on portfolio formatting and appearance, as well as how to present your portfolio to prospective employers.

Portfolio Library

www.amby.com/kimeldorf/p_mk-toc.html

> Learn all about career portfolios at this Web site from author and educator Martin Kimeldorf. Although it's geared more toward teaching professionals, anyone can adapt the concepts described here to his or her own career areas. Topics in the Portfolio Library include Using Job Search Portfolios in an Uncertain Labor Market, Life-long Learning and Education Portfolios Meet Online, Professional Development Portfolio, Portfolio Creation Tips, and more. View a sample portfolio, along with a description of how and why it was assembled.

Interviewing

After your resume has landed you that all-important job interview, you can get tips and advice on interview success from the following Web sites.

Interviewing Information

www.collegegrad.com/intv

> CollegeGrad.com is targeted at entry-level job seekers. This section of the site, packed with articles on interviewing successfully, is aimed especially at recent college graduates who might not have much interviewing experience. Get ideas on questions you can ask during interviews, check out the list of 50 standard entry-level interview questions and prepare your answers, learn how to have a successful phone interview, find out what to do after the interview, and more.

job-interview.net

www.job-interview.net

> This site provides a mix of free and for-fee information on job interviewing from the authors of *Best Answers to the 201 Most Frequently Asked Interview Questions*. Free information includes sample questions indexed by job functions, interviewing advice and tips, and a step-by-step interview success guide.

Monster: Interview Center

http://interview.monster.com

> This site is packed with informative articles on the art of being interviewed. It is organized into sections such as Land the Interview, Interview Prep, Virtual Interviews, Interview Questions, Types of Interviews, Fashion & Etiquette, Dos and Don'ts, After the Interview, and Interview Quick Tips. There's also a discussion board, which may come in handy to give you answers to specific questions.

Quintessential Careers: Guide to Job Interviewing Resources

www.quintcareers.com/intvres.html

> This collection of useful job interviewing resources includes tutorials, articles, and tools to prepare you for any type of interview. But activate your pop-up blocker first to reduce distractions. Start with the database of sample interview questions with "excellent sample responses" to find 109 of the most commonly asked questions and good ways to answer them. Take some practice interviews to see how your answers match up with the suggestions. Other great features include a job interview tutorial, a quiz to test your knowledge of the subject, and questions you can ask at an interview.

Career Clearinghouses

The collection of Web sites in this chapter can save you time. As you no
doubt know, the Web has much information about careers and jobs. It's
no surprise that a Google search for "career" produces over 762 million
results.

If you want to expand your research beyond the sites described in
other chapters of this book, there are better ways than Googling. One of
your best bets is to become familiar with the resources available at career
clearinghouses.

What Is a Clearinghouse?

A clearinghouse is an index, directory, or listing of other Internet sites.
Clearinghouses are good places to jump-start your research and save time,
because someone has already conducted Internet searches, collected the
best sites, written them up, and organized the results for you.

Clearinghouses work the same way as general Internet directories such
as Yahoo!. Because clearinghouses are usually maintained by one (or just
a few) individuals rather than by a large staff, their organization, focus,
scope, and types of sites included differ. Links generally are organized
into separate lists, allowing you to drill down easily to your desired
topic—although some (usually smaller) clearinghouses might just arrange
their links in alphabetical order. Some provide search capabilities, and others are meant simply for browsing.

Any good clearinghouse provides at least a one-line description of each linked resource—and some provide more. Clearinghouse authors also like to give their stamp of approval to selected sites. These opinions often differ. You will notice, though, that the same links are often duplicated across different clearinghouses—which can give you an idea of the major sites in a particular area, or at least those that are most highly thought of by clearinghouse authors.

Although some career clearinghouse sites strive for a comprehensive collection of resources, others are more selective and might reflect the personal bias of their author. Use your own judgment as to which type is more useful to you as you do your research. You will likely want to investigate more than one of these sites to find relevant resources, because some list sites that do not appear on others.

The Best Clearinghouses

The following list describes some of the best clearinghouses for career and job information. Use it to identify the clearinghouses that are most useful to you, and bookmark them to revisit. Then use the others to fill in when necessary.

Careers.org

www.careers.org

Careers.org consists of more than 4,000 links to career-related Internet resources, organized by category. Although it isn't as career-process-oriented as other clearinghouses, it can be a good place to search for resources for specific information. Be aware that the site makes no clear differentiation between general links and sponsored links, which try to get you to pay for services.

Internet Career Connection

http://iccweb.com

Internet Career Connection, online on AOL since 1989, is a clearinghouse of career-related information, services, and opportunities. Internet Career Connection provides searchable resource data banks for jobs in government, career counseling and coaching services, business and personal services, businesses for sale, internship and volunteer opportunities, and more. Each database listing contains a site profile you can access for further information before jumping to the resource itself.

Job-Hunt.org

www.job-hunt.org

Job-Hunt.org is owned by NETability Inc. and contains thousands of categorized, editor-selected links to career and job-hunting sites. Its posting policy contains some job-seeker-friendly criteria, including its decision not to list any sites that lack a privacy policy or that appear to be get-rich-quick or multilevel marketing scams. Each category contains annotated lists of links, the best of which are indicated by smiley-face icons. Be sure to read the introduction to each category for ideas on other sections to peruse and an explanation of the types of links you'll find included.

JobHuntersBible.com

www.jobhuntersbible.com

Dick Bolles created this Web site as a companion resource to his perennially popular book, *What Color Is Your Parachute?* Links here are divided into two major categories. The Net Guide contains a collection of information and resources for Internet job hunting. The Parachute Library is a collection of career-related articles written by Bolles and other contributors. At JobHuntersBible.com, you can take an interactive test, discover the five uses of the Internet for job seekers, create a resume and find out where to post it, search for contacts, get research tips, and a lot more. You also can learn about the latest edition of Bolles's book, including ordering information.

JobsByState.Info

www.jobsbystate.info

As the name suggests, JobsByState.Info provides a nice collection of job search resources organized by state, but it doesn't stop there. Other link categories include federal jobs; major job Web sites; newsgroups by field or region; executive/management jobs; recruiting and staffing services; job sources for women, minorities, gays and lesbians, persons with disabilities, and transitioning members of the military; and more. If you like to browse by topic rather than by alphabet, this site can save you some time.

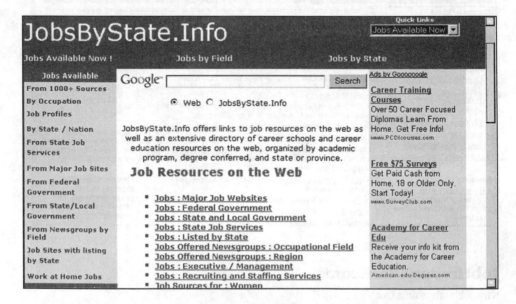

Job Searching Directory: About.com

http://jobsearch.about.com/od/findajob/

About.com features experts whose job it is to pick the best resources and create added information in the form of articles and annotations. The Job Searching Directory includes categorized links to career-related resources, from job databases to resume writing to relocation sites. Additional features include articles, forums, and a job search chat room.

Quintessential Careers

www.quintcareers.com

For an extensive list of links, visit Quintessential Careers. With over 2,400 pages of college, career, and job search information, the content will keep you coming back. New visitors should try the site tour, which explains the best ways to use the site (depending on what you're looking for). It also contains a quick-find drop-down menu, a link to a "portal" page, and a site search function, giving you several different ways to access resources. Also sign up for a free newsletter or check out the Latest Additions page to see what's been added recently.

The Riley Guide: Employment Opportunities and Job Resources on the Internet

www.rileyguide.com

One of the best and most comprehensive career and job information clearinghouses on the Internet, The Riley Guide has been online since 1994. Its simple, ad-free design is a relaxing alternative to flashier sites. The site is deep in content; the What's New page provides updates on what's been added. Pick from the major categories listed on the front page, or use the A–Z index for an alphabetical list of the thousands of resources here. Each major category is broken into subcategories, and each of these suggests other related subcategories to try. The site was created and is maintained by Margaret F. Dikel, author of *The Guide to Internet Job Searching*.

Workindex.com
www.workindex.com

Workindex.com calls itself the gateway to human resources solutions. It contains more than 5,000 Web site links for HR professionals that have been researched by the Cornell University School
of Industrial and Labor Relations. Luckily, many of these are
tremendously useful to job seekers as well! Sites are organized
into over 20 categories, and you can read a brief description of
each before visiting. You can also conduct a keyword search if
you don't find what you're looking for through the directory
index.

Researching Employer and Labor Market Information

One of the smartest things a job seeker can do is find out about an industry and an employer before walking into the interview—or, for that matter, applying for the job. Doing some research helps you make an informed decision and can leave your interviewers with an informed impression.

A number of resources help you find information on specific companies and the industries in which they operate. Read company press releases, find out the names of the key staff, scan professional journals, and get savvy about industry trends. You can find additional information through the job banks listed in chapter 4 and through the career clearinghouses described in chapter 5.

Labor market information is data about workers, industries, employers, wages, and trends. It says a lot about the changing economy, so it is of interest to many. Job seekers can take note of declining or growing occupations, along with projected employment rates for the future, before making a career move. Entrepreneurs and new-business owners research wage information when planning their staffing structure.

For more detailed information on related resources, programs, and data for your state, see the list of state employment/workforce-development agencies in chapter 4. Also note the state-based career information systems mentioned in chapter 3, which base their projections on labor market data.

Finally, don't forget about informational interviewing. Identify and talk to people in the industries or fields in which you are interested. Do some homework first so that you have some background information and can ask intelligent questions. Also, don't be shy. People who love what they do love to tell others about it, especially as they may be approaching retirement. See the section "Informational Interviewing" in chapter 3 for some how-tos on getting started.

Researching Employers

Here are some general sites for researching employers online. Remember that one of the best sources of information on a company can be its own Web site. Search for employer Web sites by using the search engines and strategies discussed in the Introduction.

CorporateInformation.com

www.corporateinformation.com

Type a company's name into the search box on the front page to find information on it. You'll see a brief analysis as well as links to articles and company profiles (often for a fee) from other Web sites. Although much information is targeted at investors, you'll find useful background material for your job hunt as well. You can also pick a state to find information on every company the site covers in that state, or you can use an alphabetical list to browse corporations. This site is best for information on large companies.

Google News

http://news.google.com

Search and browse 4,500 English-language news sources from leading search engine Google. Find the most up-to-date news stories on specific companies, or simply go to the Business section to read current articles. This is a great way to stay current on industries and specific companies. You can find out what's going on before applying or in preparation for an interview. Articles stay in the index for 30 days.

SuperPages

www.superpages.com/business/

> Verizon's SuperPages is an electronic yellow pages—with a twist. Search for U.S. businesses by keyword, name, or location, or browse by category. Each listing contains contact information as well as a Web site link when available, plus a map and driving directions. Register to create your own directory of saved listings, which you can access online from anywhere.

ThomasNet

www.thomasnet.com/

> ThomasNet is an industrial search engine designed to help industrial suppliers and buyers connect on a national, regional, and local level. You can conduct a geographic search for a product or service, a company, or a brand name, or you can browse through category listings. Check out the searchable Product News, with the latest information on industries with archives organized by category. Although the site is meant largely for locating suppliers, it's a useful way for job seekers to locate and become informed about companies in their industry as well.

Company Research Tutorials

For tips and instructions on researching employers, check out these Web sites.

Industry Research Desk

www.virtualpet.com/industry/

> Another site that emphasizes free sources, the Industry Research Desk features a 19-step process that walks you through researching a specific company or industry. This is helpful background information to have before going on that interview or applying for that position. A ton of links to useful resources are included among the steps, so take some time to explore. You'll also find ideas on print resources that can be useful; you can find many of these at your local public or college library.

Researching Companies Online

www.learnwebskills.com/company/

> Here's an online tutorial for finding no-fee company and industry information on the Web. Topics include locating company home pages, monitoring company news, learning about an industry, identifying international business resources, and researching non-profit organizations. Sounds like a sure bet for sharpening your research skills.

Riley Guide: Using the Internet to Do Job Search Research

www.rileyguide.com/jsresearch.html

> This section of the respected Riley Guide provides another useful resource for your job search, this one focusing on researching employers on the Internet. The first part provides general tips on doing effective Internet research, and the second part gives specific advice on finding company information. This step-by-step tutorial shows you how to research all aspects of your job search, and it links to a number of sites for additional information and ideas. A lot of information, uncluttered by ads.

Company Rankings

Lists are fun, and this section has a few for your viewing pleasure. A number of magazines and Web sites publish rankings of the "best" companies according to different criteria, many of which are updated yearly. Like the *U.S. News & World Report* college rankings mentioned in chapter 1, you'll want to take these light-heartedly, but they can give you an idea of what makes some organizations more highly regarded than others, and what to look for in a potential employer and why.

BestJobsUSA.com's Employers of Choice 500

www.employersofchoice.com

> BestJobsUSA.com compiles its own annual list of the best 500 companies to work for. Then it provides lists of the "Select 50" in a number of subcategories (diversity, education, healthcare, pharmaceutical, sales, and trucking). Lots of links to other ranking sites are here as well.

Fortune: 100 Best Companies to Work For

http://money.cnn.com/magazines/fortune/bestcompanies/

> *Fortune* initiated the whole company-ranking trend, and it continues to create its annual list of the 100 best companies to work for every year going back to 1998. Unfortunately, the site wants you to subscribe to the magazine (at a discounted rate) to access a lot of the information. But there's enough free info here to help you determine whether that would be a value for you.

Price's List of Lists

www.specialissues.com/lol/

> Price's List of Lists is a database of rankings of companies, people, and resources. It was started by Gary Price in 1998 and now is sponsored by SpecialIssues.com. No membership is required to browse through the lists. They show the periodical source, article name, whether the article has a fee, and the year of publication. For example, you can find the top 100 school districts and college facilities ranked by size, the top 50 propane industry retailers, and the top 100 fitness facility companies, to name just a few. The collection of periodicals that the lists are based on gives you an idea of the breadth of information covered here.

Working Mother: 100 Best Companies

www.workingwoman.com/100best.shtml

> *Working Mother* has been compiling its annual list of the 100 best companies for working mothers for over 20 years. The list provides company profiles and handy links to each company's Web

site so that you can find further information. The top ten list includes brief information on why each was selected. The Hall of Fame list includes companies that have been named to the 100 Best for 15 years or more and that appear in the current 100 Best list.

Researching Labor Market Information

Labor market information online has become more accessible and user-friendly over the years. Even better, almost all of it is made freely available by the government and other sources.

Government Sources

Most key national labor market indicators are developed by federal and state agencies. Use the government sources in this section to research industry employment estimates and projections, occupational data, labor force statistics, unemployment rates, employment hours and earnings, the consumer price index, demographic and socioeconomic data, population estimates and projections, business cycle indicators, and more. In addition, the Web sites described in this section provide information on federal programs and initiatives that affect the U.S. workforce, such as the Workforce Investment Act of 1998. If this sounds like a lot to digest, don't worry. Almost every site has search or sorting tools to help you find the information of most interest to you. To view many of the files on these sites, you need Adobe Acrobat Reader. It's available for free from the Adobe Web site at www.adobe.com/products/acrobat/readstep2.html.

FedStats

www.fedstats.gov

> If you don't know which agency keeps the statistics you need, this is a great place to begin. FedStats is the government's portal to statistics from more than 100 federal agencies. You can access the data here in a number of ways, from an A–Z index to information organized by state to a search across all these agencies' Web sites at once. You'll find an alphabetical list of agencies, with a brief description of the mission and the key types of statistics compiled by each. Check out the list of kids' pages for a fun place to start.

U.S. Bureau of Economic Analysis (BEA)

www.bea.gov

> The Bureau of Economic Analysis of the U.S. Department of Commerce is a major producer and compiler of economic, business-cycle, and labor-market data. BEA provides data and articles on regional, national, and international economic issues. Regional information includes state and local-area personal income data. National information covers personal income, the gross domestic product, corporate profits, and more. International information includes balance of payments, U.S. direct investment abroad, and foreign direct investment in the U.S. You'll also find articles that summarize and explain all this data, as well as an A–Z index, FAQs, and even a glossary.

U.S. Census Bureau

www.census.gov

The U.S. Census Bureau, another agency of the U.S. Department of Commerce, is a premiere site for socioeconomic and demographic data. Web site information is grouped into topics titled People, Business, Geography, Newsroom, and Special Topics. You can search the Web site or the FAQs by keyword. If you don't know what you're looking for, or if you want to see it all, you can browse through an alphabetical subject index. Cool stuff here includes U.S. and world population clocks, state and county profiles, economic surveys and indicators, and TIGER, the coast-to-coast digital map base. You'll definitely want to check out the American FactFinder, an interactive database tool that allows you to easily access area-specific general, social, economic, and housing statistics from Census 2000.

U.S. Census Bureau: Statistical Abstract of the United States

www.census.gov/statab/www/

The Statistical Abstract of the United States is a good example of the quantity, quality, and accessibility of information available from the U.S. Census Bureau. The section on labor force, employment, and earnings covers everything from unemployment statistics to the number of employed workers actively seeking new jobs. This information is broken down by age, sex, level of education, and occupational category. The Statistical Abstract is the resource of choice for the most useful U.S. social and economic data.

U.S. Department of Labor

www.dol.gov

The U.S. Department of Labor's Web site highlights current news. It also features quick access to popular services such as the *Occupational Outlook Handbook,* the Family and Medical Leave Act, and America's Job Bank. The site is nicely organized with links for specific audiences. One click takes you to the more than 20 links for job and training information, as well as resources for layoffs, wage and hour laws, workplace safety, retirement and health benefits, and disability information. You can use the standard search or A–Z index tools to quickly locate specific information.

U.S. Department of Labor Bureau of Labor Statistics (BLS)

www.bls.gov

The U.S. Bureau of Labor Statistics is a prime source of nationwide labor market information. It also has a significant amount of information at the state and local level. BLS has extensive Internet offerings, including inflation and consumer spending, employment and unemployment statistics, a variety of productivity indexes, employee benefits and compensation surveys, and even career information for kids. You can also access regional BLS offices for information targeted to your area to get statistics on the regional economy by state and metropolitan area (such as the current unemployment rate in your city or employment statistics by industry). This site is searchable and contains an A–Z index to help you find needed information. Or you can drill down through the categories listed on the front page (including demographics, occupations, wages, earnings, benefits, and more) to locate your specific topic of interest.

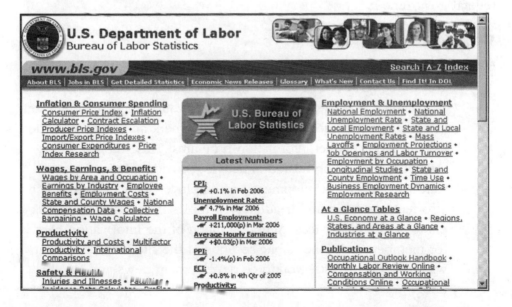

U.S. Department of Labor Employment and Training Administration (ETA)

www.doleta.gov

The U.S. Department of Labor Employment and Training Administration is the primary agency for federal workforce development programs. Much of the Web site content is aimed at federal and state professionals working in employment and training programs. But if you're a job seeker, check out the Advancing Your Career section for resources to help you start a new job, make long-term career plans, research job opportunities, deal with job loss, and find training to acquire new skills. Employers can get information on government incentives and assistance and employment resources. You'll also find links to state and local resources such as one-stop centers, training providers, and more.

Workforce Development

Workforce development concerns initiatives and programs addressing the growth and maintenance of an educated, skilled workforce. These programs typically are coordinated among multiple public, private, and nonprofit employment and training providers and are funded through the federal government.

Workforce ATM

www.icesa.org

Workforce ATM is a service of the National Association of State Work Force Agencies, the national organization of state administrators of unemployment insurance, employment and training services, and labor market information programs. This Web site helps track information on related initiatives, providing links to each state's workforce development and employer services agencies. It also features news and headlines on topics from dislocated workers to veterans' services. Although much of the information here is for members only, the public sections of the site provide a great way to keep up with workforce development news and information.

Military Careers

The U.S. military is one of the country's largest employers, including service members on full-time active duty, part-time reservists, and National Guard members. Each year, the military hires over 365,000 new enlisted and officer personnel.

Learn about the wide variety of military career options by exploring the sites in this chapter, which describe military recruiting, the different branches, service academies, reserves and the National Guard, civilian job opportunities, and even resources for military spouses. You'll also find sites that will be helpful as you make the jump back to civilian employment after your military career.

In addition to helping you learn whether the military is for you, the information at these sites can get you up to speed before you sit down to talk to a recruiter. Doing your research always pays off.

Beyond the learning opportunities that serving in the military offers, the military also sponsors a number of lifelong and distance learning options for current and retired service members. You can find information on these programs in chapter 2.

General Information

About the U.S. Military

http://usmilitary.about.com

About.com scores again with a wide collection of military resources from current news to recruitment, pay and benefits, off-duty information, and life after the military. Sign up for a free weekly e-newsletter, see the glossary of military terms, get answers to FAQs, and peruse the list of how-tos (such as how to survive boot camp or how to ship your vehicle overseas).

ASVAB Career Exploration Program

http://asvabprogram.com

The ASVAB's (Armed Services Vocational Aptitude Battery) main purpose is to show students and potential recruits where their aptitudes and abilities lie, helping them make the best military, educational, and career choices. This comprehensive site supports the ASVAB Career Exploration Program, which is used in many schools to help students make these choices. All new recruits must take the exam to determine which military careers they are eligible for.

Military.com

www.military.com

Military.com claims to be the largest online military destination. Unique offerings here include a buddy finder and community center, a military scholarship database, a veterans job board, a military mentor network, military news, a military reunion planning guide and posting service, and even a place to post your personal blog. How to join the military is spelled out for you in a ten-step process, with recruiter links, an ASVAB practice test, and discussion boards offering firsthand advice and knowledge. And if you get tired of reading, you can visit the photo and video gallery.

My Future

www.myfuture.com

Here you can sign up to receive more information on branches of the service that interest you, take work interest and personality quizzes, and find out about military education funding. This Web site has information on general career exploration, job search techniques, and money management, but its strength lies in the military career information. Learn about skills training and educational opportunities, and get answers to common military questions. It's a good stop on the research trail for someone considering a military career.

Stars and Stripes

www.stripes.com

To get a sense of being in the military, read what U.S. military personnel are reading. *Stars and Stripes* is a Department of Defense–authorized daily newspaper distributed overseas for the U.S. military community. Editorially independent of interference from outside its editorial chain of command, it provides commercially available U.S. and world news and objective staff-produced stories relevant to the military community in a balanced, fair, and accurate manner. Your knowledge of current military events is sure to impress a recruiter.

Today's Military

www.todaysmilitary.com

Today's Military is a good first stop if you (or your son or daughter) are considering a career in the military. Formerly the Military Career Guide Online, this site provides general information on military life and the rewards of a military career. In addition, you can browse through officer and enlisted jobs organized by career category. Each description includes information on areas such as duties, helpful attributes, training provided, and work environment. This site is also available in Spanish.

U.S. Military Branches of Service

Air Force

Air Force Link/Careers

www.af.mil/careers/

Information on careers for enlisted personnel, officers, civilians, and retirees can be found in the Careers section of Air Force Link, the official Web site for the Air Force. Look through current employment opportunities and find out about pay scales, promotions, retirement pay, and all the other details of an Air Force career. For plenty more Air Force information, visit other sections of Air Force Link, including News, TV, Radio, Photos, Letters, History, and more.

U.S. Air Force

www.airforce.com

This official recruiting Web site for the U.S. Air Force requires the latest Macromedia Flash and other multimedia plugins to capture the excitement of an Air Force career. Browse through career fields by category to find the one that's right for you, and find out about all the benefits of an Air Force career. You can also sign up to receive more information, chat online with an advisor, or view videos of Air Force operations and personnel.

Army

GoArmy.com

www.goarmy.com

The official U.S. Army recruiting site provides an overview of Army life through articles, photos, and video interviews. Browse job categories or search for a specific career. Learn about enlistment incentives, officer training, college education benefits, and specialized opportunities such as the Army Band, Chaplain Corps, Judge Advocate General's Corps, and Special Forces. Chat with a recruiter online, or send for additional information.

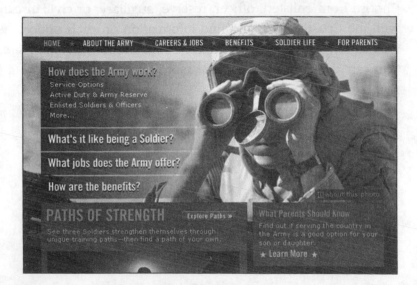

U.S. Army

www.army.mil

The official U.S. Army site includes tons of information for anyone interested in an Army career. You could spend hours browsing through the news and links here, or search for the specific information you need. Pick the Career Management link to find out about Army careers, including enlisted, officer, and civilian opportunities.

Coast Guard

U.S. Coast Guard

www.uscg.mil/USCG.shtm

Part of the U.S. Department of Homeland Security, the Coast Guard provides links on its official site to news, jobs, services, history, Coast Guard missions, and more. Its motto is "Semper Paratus" (Always Ready). This site provides all the details you need about this service branch.

U.S. Coast Guard Recruiting

www.gocoastguard.com

Choose from enlisted, officer, reserve, auxiliary, or civilian careers with the Coast Guard, and find information on each option, as well as scholarship opportunities, at this official recruiting site. You can also sign up to receive more information or locate a recruiter near you.

Marines

Marines.com

www.marines.com

> Marines.com is the official recruiting site for the U.S. Marine Corps, and it features visual images of the Marine Corps. You have a choice of the Flash version, requiring browser plugin software, or the standard version, which is more directly linked to information. Find out here about training, job opportunities, educational options, Marine history and heritage, and more.

U.S. Marine Corps

www.usmc.mil

> The official Marine Corps Web site covers all things Marine, from the band to news to history, video, and images of the Corps. Search for a desired topic, or simply browse the main page for links to current stories and information. There's plenty to keep you coming back.

Navy

U.S. Navy

www.navy.mil

> Welcome aboard the official U.S. Navy Web site, your one-stop shop for information on everything from careers to ships. Get briefed on the latest Navy news on the home page. For specific information, the site index and site search are your doorways to finding all the facts you need. You also can click Got a Question? for FAQs and answers.

U.S. Navy Opportunities

www.navyjobs.com

> "Accelerate your life" at the Navy's official recruitment site. If a military career is in your future, speed up your search by exploring all the information here, including an online self-assessment and descriptions of Navy careers, benefits, and educational opportunities. Get answers to your specific questions through the message board, which has a special thread for parents.

U.S. Service Academies

The service academies give you a four-year college education while preparing you for a career as an officer in the armed forces. Strict admissions guidelines consider such factors as U.S. citizenship (with certain exceptions), academic performance, standardized test scores, extracurricular activities, athletic ability, age, marital status, and moral character. All but the Coast Guard Academy require that you be nominated by a member of Congress or another qualified nominator.

Air Force Academy Admissions Center

http://academyadmissions.com

> Geared specifically toward students (and their parents), this well-organized site walks you through all aspects of applying for admission to the U.S. Air Force Academy, from finding out about academic majors to applying online. Parents will appreciate the parents' guide, full of information to help them understand what the Academy has to offer their son or daughter.

U.S. Air Force Academy

www.usafa.af.mil

> This official site of the U.S. Air Force Academy in Colorado Springs, Colorado, offers information on all aspects of student life, academics, and programs. Highlights include a home page packed with the latest academy news, information for visitors, descriptions and a photo gallery of cadet life, and much more.

U.S. Coast Guard Academy

www.cga.edu

Learn all about the Coast Guard Academy in New London, Connecticut, at its official Web site. The Prospective Cadet link leads to quick information on the Academy, from an overview to an online application form to FAQs. News, history, candidate profiles, and information on cadet life and academics can help you decide whether there's a Coast Guard career in your future.

U.S. Merchant Marine Academy

www.usmma.edu

Find out what it takes to be admitted to the U.S. Merchant Marine Academy at Kings Point, New York. Read online about admissions, academic requirements, midshipman life, athletics, and more. Or browse the downloadable .pdf catalog to read at your leisure.

U.S. Military Academy (West Point)

www.usma.edu

Current news events are featured on the home page of the U.S. Military Academy. To learn about its 200-year tradition, start with About the Academy to explore its programs, including academic, physical, military, and moral-ethical components. A site search and FAQs help you drill down to the information you need.

U.S. Naval Academy

www.nadn.navy.mil

This is the official site for the U.S. Naval Academy in Annapolis, Maryland. Browse through the announcements and links listed here, or use the search or site index to find specific information. Admissions information includes a handy step-by-step description of the process to help you become a well-prepared applicant.

National Guard

The National Guard serves the dual mission of supporting the armed forces in times of war and maintaining order at a state level during emergencies. Find out about the different branches and about full- and part-time soldier and civilian opportunities at the sites described here. Read through the primary Guard sites described in this section for good, general information, and then visit the recruiting sites for specifics on signing up.

Air National Guard

Air National Guard (ANG)

www.ang.af.mil

> If your future is up in the air, the Air National Guard may provide some options. This official site of the Air National Guard includes recruiting information, the history of the ANG, full-time and part-time career opportunities, and links to ANG units across the country.

Air National Guard Recruitment

www.goang.com

> Explore recruiting information and career opportunities with the Air National Guard, get questions answered through an online chat, request information from your local recruiter, and find out the benefits that even a part-time Air National Guard career can bring. You can also search for open positions by state or keyword, get the real scoop on basic training, or take a break in the online arcade.

Army National Guard

Army National Guard

www.arng.ngb.army.mil

> The Army National Guard is one component of the Army, which consists of the active Army (described earlier), the Army National Guard, and the Army Reserve (described in the next section). This official site describes the Guard's unique dual mission of both federal and state roles, as well as extensive information on the Guard's organization, current activities, leadership, and history. Use the site map to move around the site easily and zero in on the information you want.

Army National Guard Recruitment

www.1800goguard.com

> The official Army National Guard online recruiting center includes information for students and graduates, veterans, medical professionals, parents, and educators. Find out about the history of the Guard, learn about basic and career training, and get the lowdown on money for college as well as salary and benefit information. Use a quick link to contact a recruiter or sign up for e-mail Guard updates.

The Reserves

The Armed Forces Reserves are military personnel who are not normally on full-time active duty but who are trained and equipped to be mobilized during a war or national crisis. High school graduates can apply to ROTC (Reserve Officer Training Corps) programs to earn a college education while also receiving officer training in their military branch.

Air Force

U.S. Air Force Reserve

www.afreserve.com

> Explore the missions of the U.S. Air Force Reserve at its official
> Web site. Site tools include a recruiter locator, live chat, FAQs,
> game and screen-saver downloads, a site map, and a special sec-
> tion for parents. A wide range of information is available here,
> from the benefits of joining the Air Force Reserve to reports on air
> show events and Air Force Reserve Touring Car racing.

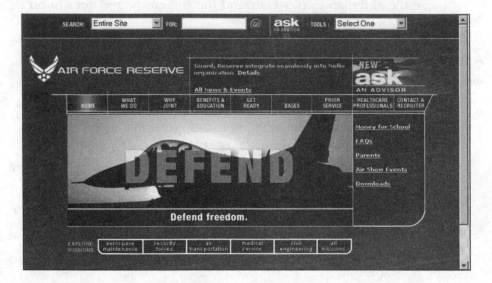

U.S. Air Force Reserve Officer Training Corps (ROTC)

www.afrotc.com

> More than 1,000 U.S. colleges and universities participate in the
> Air Force ROTC program. Through the program, you can get the
> money you need for college and earn a degree while working
> toward becoming an officer in the U.S. Air Force. Get information
> on the program, read about admissions standards and require-
> ments, or apply online for a scholarship. Videos of individual
> cadets give you an idea of what the program is like, and you can
> explore Air Force careers to see what opportunities await you
> after graduation.

Army

U.S. Army Reserve

www.goarmy.com/reserve/nps/

Get an in-depth look at the types of training you can receive as an Army Reserve soldier; learn about education benefits, cash bonuses, and lifestyle benefits; read a featured profile of a reservist; and find out what Reserve jobs are available to you. You can chat online with a recruiter or contact one locally, e-mail a question, or request an information packet be sent to you.

U.S. Army Reserve Officer Training Corps (ROTC)

www.goarmy.com/rotc/

Army ROTC is an elective curriculum you take along with your required college classes. Army ROTC offers two-, three-, and four-year college scholarships to qualified high school seniors or current college students, plus you graduate into an Army career with a rank of Second Lieutenant. Get all the specifics here and learn from the experiences of officers who launched their Army careers through the program.

Coast Guard

U.S. Coast Guard Reserve

www.uscg.mil/reserve/

Get the whole story on the U.S. Coast Guard Reserve as well as recruiting information. Here you can read *The Reservist* and *Coast Guard* magazines, keep up on current events, and learn about training opportunities, including the Reserve Enlisted Basic Indoctrination (REBI) course in Cape May, New Jersey.

Navy

U.S. Navy Reserve

www.navyreserve.com

> The top five reasons people join the Navy Reserve are patriotism, career advancement, camaraderie, leadership skills, and physical fitness. If you identify with these, find out more here about entry requirements, entrance programs, enlisted and officer opportunities, pay, and benefits. Profiles of current reservists provide great information on actual experiences in the Reserve.

U.S. Navy Reserve Officer Training Corps (NROTC)

https://www.nrotc.navy.mil

> If you aspire to be a naval aviator, flight officer, special warfare officer, submarine officer, or surface warfare officer, the NROTC may be your career ticket. Successful applicants are awarded scholarships through a highly competitive national selection process. They receive full tuition, books, fees, and other financial benefits at many of the country's leading colleges and universities. Upon graduation, students become commissioned officers. This site describes the full range of career options. After you have applied, you can revisit this site to check your application's status.

Civilian Opportunities in (or for) the Military

Soldiers are not the only contributors to the effectiveness of our armed forces. Check out the numbers of civilians employed to appreciate this job market. The military relies on civilian employees to fulfill roles not covered through military positions. Find out here about civilian positions you may not have known existed.

Air Force Personnel Center (AFPC) Civilian Employment

https://ww2.afpc.randolph.af.mil/resweb/

> This page is designed to be a one-stop shopping list for civilian employees and job seekers. A great time-saver, it clearly describes what services are available to job seekers through the Air Force Personnel Center. The Air Force employs over 150,000 civilians in a full range of occupations, including financial management, information management, public affairs, engineering, computers/communications, sports/fitness recreation management, contracting, logistics, and education, to name a few. Expand your career options and thinking by poking around here.

Army and Air Force Exchange Service (AAFES) Employment Opportunities

http://odin.aafes.com/Employment/default.asp

> AAFES employs over 50,000 civilians in base or post exchanges on U.S. military installations worldwide. AAFES recruits for entry-level and management positions in retail, information systems, finance and accounting, logistics, food service/restaurant management, contracting and procurement, and occasionally other career fields. If you're married to an active-duty military member, you may qualify for a spouse employment hiring preference.

Army Civilian Personnel On-Line

http://cpol.army.mil

> Civilians have been working for the U.S. military since the Revolutionary War. In today's Army, they work in a wide range of occupations, including scientist, engineer, administrator, physician, information technologist, childcare director, program analyst, recreation specialist, customer service representative, and many more. The site lets you search for vacancy announcements by keyword, location, general occupation, and pay grade. You can also submit an electronic resume with the site's Resume Builder program, with online help provided.

Civilian On-line Applicant Staffing Tool (COAST)

www.uscg.mil/hq/cgpc/cpm/jobs/vacancy.htm

Over 6,000 civilian jobs exist in the U.S. Coast Guard, including professional, administrative, technical, trades and labor, full-time, part-time, and student positions. Search current job openings, and use the automated application system to receive e-mail notifications of new job openings and apply for them.

Department of the Navy's Civilian Hiring and Recruitment Tool

https://chart.donhr.navy.mil

What could a librarian in Sicily, a pharmacist in Oak Harbor, Washington, and a social worker in Spain have in common? They may all be civilian employees of the U.S. Navy or Marine Corps. According to the Department of Navy Civilian Human Resources, over 182,000 civilians are employed in Naval and Marine Corps activities throughout the world. Get the scoop on the jobs at this site with its searchable job opportunity database. Then create a personal account to use the resume builder and create automated job search agents.

Especially for Spouses

Being in the military is more than a job—it's a way of life, as any military spouse will confirm. For many, that includes working. These sites are geared to the unique and specific needs of military families.

Military Spouse Career Center

www.military.com/spouse

Take steps to your own career success by starting at Military Spouse Career Center. Here you can read job hunting tips, search for jobs, find family support resources, and connect with others through discussion boards and a newsletter. Plus, if you create an account, you can post your resume online and get updates on the latest listings. The Military Spouse Career Center Web site is operated by Monster and Military.com under contract with the Department of Defense, so the amount of information and number of resources here should come as no surprise.

MilSpouse.org

www.milspouse.org

If you are married to the military, this is the site for you. MilSpouse.org is a clearinghouse of employment, education, and relocation information and resources addressing the special needs of military families. It's sponsored by the Department of Defense and the Department of Labor. Locate your military base welcome center, get tips on preparing for a job campaign, learn about educational opportunities, find out where you can turn for relocation assistance—it's all here.

MyArmyLifeToo.com

www.myarmylifetoo.com

This site aims to be the "Web site of choice for Army families," and you'll find plenty to back that up. The topics range from work and careers to lifelong learning, money matters, home and family life, and managing deployment. You can also find specific resources based on whether your spouse is a member of the active Army, the Army National Guard, or the Army Reserve.

Post-Military Careers

Military and government-funded employment assistance programs help active military personnel make the jump back into civilian employment. In addition, other organizations have stepped in to help connect veterans with employers. All of them are putting the power of the Internet to work to make information and services readily available and accessible.

Corporate Gray Online

www.greentogray.com

Corporate Gray Online exists for one purpose: to provide free military transition services for veterans. Employers that use Corporate Gray Online understand the military environment and search the database of online resumes for job candidates with the mix of skills and experience that fits their needs. Post your resume to apply online with hundreds of "military-friendly" companies, or make an in-person visit to one of the military job fairs that Corporate Gray sponsors across the U.S. You can also sign up to have new job listings matching your criteria sent to your e-mail inbox. If that's not enough, you can find training and educational opportunities for veterans, as well as helpful tips on relocation, links to sites for doing company research, FAQs, and other job search resources.

Department of Defense (DoD) TransPortal

www.dodtransportal.org

This portal for transitioning military provides information on DoD transition assistance services, including contact information for the different branches, a preseparation guide, and mini-courses on conducting a job search and applying for jobs online. You can also find links to Internet job search sites and corporate recruiting sites.

elaws Advisors: Veterans' Issues

www.dol.gov/elaws/veterans.html

The elaws Advisors from the U.S. Department of Labor are interactive e-tools that provide easy-to-understand information about a number of federal employment laws as well as other helpful information. Veterans' Issues explains federal laws on reemployment rights, veterans' preference, and federal contract compliance. In addition, the e-VETS Resource Advisor provides a list of Web sites most relevant to your specific needs and interests, such as job search tools and tips, employment openings, career assessment, education and training, and benefits and special services available to veterans. The REALifelines Advisor is designed to help wounded and injured veterans find online resources and contact information for one-on-one employment assistance.

Transition Assistance Online

www.taonline.com

About 200,000 service members each year transition from active duty. If you're among them, or if you're among the thousands of veterans, reservists, retirees, guardsmen, and working spouses who are looking for new civilian jobs and other career opportunities, this site is for you. After setting up a free account, you can not only search for job openings using multiple search criteria, but you also can use the online resume and resume management tools. Furthermore, you can sign up for an electronic newsletter that provides information on job-seeker services for the military community.

Veteran Career Network

http://benefits.military.com/vcn/search.do

The goal of the Veteran Career Network is to help veterans capitalize on the training they received in the military by connecting them with employers that value this type of training. You can view the career profiles of other veterans in the network; contact network members in specific companies, locations, or careers; or post your own profile for others to view. You can also conduct a job search, post a resume, and use the skills translator to translate your MOS, Rate, AFSC, or designator into civilian terms. The Veteran Career Network, from Military.com, opened its doors, appropriately enough, on Veterans' Day in 2005.

Veterans' Employment and Training Service (VETS)

www.dol.gov/vets/

All veterans should be aware of the Veterans' Employment and Training Service (VETS) in the U.S. Department of Labor, the federal agency working on their behalf. That said, information of most interest to the individual is better found at elaws Advisors: Veterans' Issues (described earlier in this section). What you will find here are descriptions on the programs, laws, and regulations administered by the agency.

VetJobs.com

www.vetjobs.com

VetJobs.com helps vets understand how to approach the civilian job market and helps employers appreciate veterans' skills and capabilities. Search the jobs database, or post your resume online to let potential employers find you. You can also subscribe to a free monthly e-mail newsletter to get tips on using the site and making the transition. Also check out resources and organizations for additional support, or see the employment assistance category for tips on interviewing and job hunting in the civilian sector. The site has the exclusive endorsement of the U.S. Veterans of Foreign Wars (VFW).

Self-Employment and Small Business

Thinking about self-employment? You're far from alone. According to the U.S. Census Bureau, over 10.5 million Americans are self-employed, 40 percent of them in management, professional, and related occupations.

Many self-employed people start the process by working as a free agent or contractor and then extend the concept to create their own business. (For more on free agency, see chapter 9.) Whether you work from home as a "SOHO-ist" (we'll explain later) or create a business that grows to employ tens or hundreds of people, owning your own business puts you in control of your employment. Independence is the most common reason cited for going the self-employment route.

Being self-employed, however, doesn't mean you have to go it alone. These days you can join a networking group or professional association, receive free e-newsletters, read business magazines online, locate an e-mail or face-to-face mentor, find specific information for little or no cost, post questions or comments in discussion groups, chat online with others like yourself, or participate in a live telediscussion.

The Web sites in this chapter provide you with convenient, quality information not only to help you make good business decisions but also to connect you with others and stay informed, motivated, and inspired.

Government Resources for Small Businesses

What did we do before the Internet, especially when it comes to finding government information? Federal, state, and local government has gotten much better at using the Internet to make the information we need easier to find. This is especially good news for business owners sorting their way through regulations and requirements.

Business.gov

www.business.gov

> Visit Business.gov for one-stop access to federal information and services. Mine for information either by phase (Launching, Managing, Growing, Getting Out), by topic (ranging from Business Laws to International Trade), or by keyword search. Because more than 22 federal organizations assist or regulate U.S. businesses, this site can save you a lot of time. The searchable FAQs include information from all these organizations. Everything from paying taxes and financing a business to selling your goods and services to the government is covered here.

Internal Revenue Service (IRS)

www.irs.gov/businesses/small/

> When you become self-employed or open a business, the complexity of your taxes can change dramatically. The IRS's business center includes a section devoted to small businesses and the self-employed. It should be one of your first stops as you begin to plan. View a streaming video of an IRS small-business workshop, take an IRS course, or complete an online self-directed version of a workshop taught live around the country. Or find downloadable forms and publications, learn about electronic filing, browse small-business news stories and tax-law changes, and more.

SCORE: Counselors to America's Small Business

www.score.org

> The 10,500 members of SCORE, the Service Corps of Retired Executives, provide free and confidential e-mail and in-person small-business mentoring and advice. Use this site to locate an office near you, or search for an e-mail counselor whose skills match your needs. You'll also find success stories, articles, information and links on starting a business, free planning workbooks, and free e-mail newsletters on resources and entrepreneurial issues.

State and Local Government on the Net

www.statelocalgov.net

> Don't forget to check with state and local agencies for business regulations and requirements in your location. Fortunately, this handy directory helps you find those agencies in a few clicks. For most states, look for the department of commerce under the executive branch listings.

U.S. Small Business Administration (SBA)

www.sbaonline.sba.gov

> The SBA is one of your best stops on the road to self-employment. Plan to visit often—there's too much to grasp in one visit. To help you find your way around, the site is organized into the general topics of starting, financing, and managing your business, along with business opportunities and disaster recovery. The Starting Your Business section includes information on planning, marketing, and employment, as well as an online Small Business Startup Guide (which you can also order in print form from your local SBA office). Locate your local office, browse FAQs for answers to the questions that aspiring small-business owners most often ask, and find detailed information on common tasks such as creating your business plan. Other features include online chats, an e-newsletter, and information on training opportunities. This site is also available in Spanish.

Small-Business Solutions

The Web sites in this section provide a mix of information and services for new and experienced entrepreneurs. Start-up business owners will appreciate the getting-started information about writing business plans and the like. Experienced entrepreneurs looking for new business trends, new marketing channels, or just new ideas won't be disappointed either.

About.com: Small Business Information

http://sbinformation.about.com

> Although About.com is unfortunately heavy on distracting advertising, this site offers extensive information for small-business owners (and aspiring owners). Subscribe to a free e-mail newsletter, join the discussion forum, read featured articles, learn about business blogging, or select a topic of interest from the subject links here. Each subject link contains a number of links to useful sites on the topic. Subjects range from writing business plans to economic trends.

AllBusiness.com

www.allbusiness.com

> With how-to articles, business forms, contracts and agreements, expert advice, blogs, business news, business directory listings, product comparisons, business guides, and more, AllBusiness.com just might become your go-to site for business questions. Topics here range from business plans, consulting, and incorporating to personal finance, sales and marketing, and technology. In addition, free registration gives you full access to the AllBusiness.com periodicals library of more than 700,000 articles from 400 leading business and industry publications plus a choice of free subscriptions to e-newsletters.

Bplans.com

www.bplans.com

> You need a business plan before you can get financing for your new business—not to mention the need to clarify your plans and prospects before starting. Learn by example at Bplans.com, which provides 60 sample business plans for free online viewing. Bplans.com is a free service from Palo Alto Software, Inc., which produces software products for small business. Other freebies here include interactive tools to walk you through calculating starting costs, finding financing options, and creating an initial assessment for your business plan. The site also includes expert answers to questions on business and marketing plans, planning software and entrepreneuring, and articles on starting and managing a business.

Business Owners' Idea Café

www.businessownersideacafe.com

> For "a fun approach to serious business," visit the Business Owners' Idea Café. Interact with other entrepreneurs and experts in the Cyberschmooz area, find tons of resources for starting and running a small business, and relax in specialized sections for Generation X and work-at-home moms. Free registration gives you access to the small-business grant center, newsletter, contests,

opportunities to promote your business, and more. Although the approach might be casual, the advice is anything but. You'll find a lot of useful information in a quick and friendly format.

CCH Business Owner's Toolkit

www.toolkit.cch.com

The Toolkit offers a great deal of useful information and tools to let you start and run your own successful business, from experts who know their stuff. Scroll down to see the different categories in the small-business guide, ranging from writing a business plan to hiring the right people. You'll also find free downloadable business tools, including sample policies and forms that you can use and/or modify for your own purposes. Also check out the Ask Alice! advice column for Q&A on small-business issues. The Toolkit is a free service of CCH Tax and Accounting, a provider of business, legal, and tax information and software.

How to Start a Small Business

http://sbdc.deltacollege.org/startup/

An online book and award-winning Web site in one, this site from the San Joaquin Delta College Small Business Development Center is full of information and resources on starting your own business. Start with the table of contents to get a breakdown of the topics covered here, or read straight through for complete coverage of all the steps involved. Each section includes links to additional articles, information, and sites. An interactive index allows you to locate the specific information you need with just a click. Even better, there are no ads, and no registration is required for full site access. This site is also available in Spanish.

Network Solutions

www.networksolutions.com

Thinking about getting your own domain name for a Web site? Find out if your first choice is available by searching the database at Network Solutions. The granddaddy of domain registrars, Network Solutions is now only one of many domain name registration services. For more (and often cheaper) options, see the Accredited Registrar Directory from ICANN, the Internet Corporation for Assigned Names and Numbers, at www.internic.net/regist.html.

Nolo.com

www.nolo.com

Nolo is the name for legal information for the busy small-business owner on a budget, whether you're dealing with business and human resources; patents, copyright, and art; wills and estate planning; property and money; family law and immigration; or rights and disputes. Read articles, get advice, and use action step checklists or interactive calculators. You can also locate and purchase helpful do-it-yourself legal titles and software from Nolo if you need further information or print references. Some background reading here may provide what you need or help you fine-tune your questions to take to your clock-watching attorney.

Operating Your Successful Small Business

http://sbdc.deltacollege.org/inbusiness/

Here's another online book from the San Joaquin Delta College Small Business Development Center. This one's about keeping your business afloat and on course after a successful launch. Browse the table of contents for topics of interest, or find specific information through the index. A list of other online resources is organized into categories such as commercial enterprises, directories, employees, government contracting, and inventions. As with How to Start a Business (discussed earlier in this section), you see no ads, and you don't register for access to the information.

Seed Business Network

www.seedbiznet.org

Seed Business Network aims to be a one-stop destination for disability employment, self-employment for people with disabilities, disability resources, disability consulting, and business life coaching for the disabled. Sign up for the free e-newsletter, or become a member for a nominal fee. Under Resources, find articles and links to other information organized under Business, Disability, Health, and Computer. Future plans call for business and health forums, business-related blogs, webinars, interactive workbooks, and a bulletin board.

Small Business Advisor

www.isquare.com

Plenty of current information is available here at Small Business Advisor. Start with the advice for first-time visitors to learn how to optimize your time at this site, or visit the site map for the full picture. You can choose from nearly 100 articles on topics such as starting and operating a business, sales, marketing, legal matters, and dealing with customers. Other features include handy checklists, book reviews, tips on marketing and taxes, a glossary of small-business terms, and links to other resources.

Franchises

Franchises provide a ready-made business opportunity for those who want to start their own business with the security of an established brand behind their efforts. The sites in this section cover places to find franchise opportunities and discuss franchising in general.

BISON: The Franchise Network

www.bison1.com

If you're thinking of buying a franchise, BISON can steer you in some helpful directions. BISON (for Business International Sales and Opportunity Network) strives to provide comprehensive information on franchising, so there is a lot to explore here. Search here for franchise opportunities by subject, and find information on each company, including costs. Each includes a link to request more information (but note that your net worth and liquid capital are required). You'll also find franchising news, profiles of featured franchises, and financing options.

Entrepreneur.com Franchise Zone

www.entrepreneur.com/Franchise_Zone/

> On this portal for franchisers, you'll find news, advice, articles, and assistance. The franchise directory contains categorized opportunities. The information on each company includes investment requirements, fees, and funding information; background and contact information; information on franchise growth; where the company stands in *Entrepreneur* magazine's franchise rankings; the type of training and support the company provides; and suggestions on where it is seeking franchisees. For more reading, click the link to *Franchise Zone* magazine for articles, tips, and how-tos.

Franchising.com

www.franchising.com

> Is franchising for you? At Franchising.com you can learn how to make the franchising decision, be a successful franchisee, and find the franchise opportunity that's right for you. The site provides detailed information about various franchising and business opportunities, insightful articles, a directory of franchise attorneys, and other franchising resources.

Online Business Magazines

The energy is high at these online business magazines. Online publications make keeping "in the know" quick and convenient. And with the searchable magazine archives, there's no longer a need for you to keep back issues.

CNNMoney.com

http://money.cnn.com/

CNNMoney.com is the Internet home for four popular business and financial magazines: *Fortune, Money, Business 2.0,* and *Fortune Small Business*. You can read the entire contents of the magazines—including back issues—for free online, or you can search one or all for specific words or phrases. No registration is required unless you want to subscribe to an e-newsletter, and there are several to choose from.

Entrepreneur.com

www.entrepreneur.com

Anything you could want to know about small business you can probably find here, either by browsing the 11 categories, looking it up in the business encyclopedia, or conducting a keyword search. Upper-level topics include Startups, HomeBiz, Franchise, BizOpps, Money, Marketing, Manage, EBiz, Tech, Work/Life, and Grow Your Biz. Each is full of articles, how-tos, success stories, and lots of ideas and advice. If that's not enough, you can read the current and past issues of *Entrepreneur* and *Be Your Own Boss* magazines.

Fast Company

www.fastcompany.com

> *Fast Company* wants to be the first word in cutting-edge business thinking, and the magazine has made waves since its launch in 1997. The Web site's content is generous, with every article in every issue (except the current issue) archived online, searchable, and conveniently organized by topic. Fast Company Online Guides are editor-selected collections of the best articles on the Internet and technology, leadership, marketing and branding, sales and customer service, strategy and innovation, and more. If you like blogging, you can read not only FC Now, the *Fast Company* blog, but also choose from over 50 others.

Inc.com

www.inc.com

> Browse through Inc.com's collection of articles organized by topics such as finance and capital, technology, leadership, e-commerce, law and taxation, and much more, as you might

expect from a leading business magazine. Check out the current issue's table of contents, or get lots of how-to advice on everything from finding and retaining customers to gearing up for tax time. With a free Inc.com membership, you get access to more than 100 free tools, such as interactive worksheets and a choice of 11 free e-mail newsletters.

Business Associations

Business associations are a great place to network with other small-business owners, get ideas, find resources, and build new business opportunities. This section contains some Web sites of general associations to get you started. Also consider associations focusing on your business's specialty.

National Association for the Self-Employed (NASE)
www.nase.org

NASE focuses exclusively on the needs of "micro-businesses"—those with no more than 10 employees. NASE aims to help members tackle issues such as business financing and affordable health care through providing how-to resources, access to a wide range of professional services at discounted rates, and legislative advocacy. NASE members have access to ShopTalk800, a toll-free help line, but anyone can browse the micro-business topics or sign up to receive the "Get Connected" e-newsletter.

National Federation of Independent Business (NFIB)
www.nfib.com

NFIB is a large advocacy organization for small business, with a membership of over 600,000 businesses. Learn about state and national issues facing small-business owners, search the database of business articles for practical information and tips for small-business owners, and find out about member benefits. Member benefits are similar to those for NASE, including health, travel, service, and other discounts.

U.S. Chamber of Commerce

www.uschamber.com

As you establish your small business, consider taking advantage of the services of your local Chamber of Commerce. Chambers provide members with invaluable networking opportunities, business contacts, and business education options. Use the Chamber Directory at this site to locate your Chamber and to link directly to its Web site (when available) for more information. The U.S. Chamber of Commerce site also includes news, events, member benefits, and advocacy information.

SOHO: Small Office/Home Office

Almost 20 million Americans now work at least one day a week from home, either through a telecommuting/freelance arrangement with outside employers or in their own home-based business. The work-at-home trend continues so strongly that it's become a market segment with its own catchy acronym: SOHO (small office/home office). The Web sites in this section cover the work-at-home lifestyle in general. For information on telecommuting, contracting, and freelancing, see chapter 9.

Aardvarks Home Workers Association

www.ahwa.com

If you want to work from home but you're not interested in starting a business, Aardvarks offers you options—for a fee. Search
through directories of home-based jobs, subscribe to the job listing
newsletters to receive the latest listings, or create and post your
resume. Complete medical, dental, optical, and legal benefits programs are available through Aardvarks, plus over 1,000 downloadable publications. Aardvarks offers a money-back guarantee to
help you evaluate all the site's resources risk-free.

The Entrepreneurial Parent

http://en-parent.com/

The Entrepreneurial Parent is a work-family resource for home-
office entrepreneurs and career professionals who are looking for
alternative work options. If you aspire to grow your family and
your career under one roof while staying connected to others,
check out the resources available here, including articles organized by topics. Your Family covers parenting and childcare and
includes firsthand accounts from entrepreneurial parents. Your
Career features advice from career counselors. Your Business provides a wide variety of advice, tools, exercises, and insights to
help you start, manage, and grow your home business. Ask the EP
experts for guidance, subscribe to the free e-newsletter, or participate in a discussion forum.

A Home-Based Business Online (AHBBO)

www.ahbbo.com

If you're hunting for a home-based business idea, check out the
master list of ideas at AHBBO. Detailed information on 130 businesses is also available for download for a fee. Subscribe to the
AHBBO e-zine and get caught up by reading the archives of past
issues. Be sure to check out the article library, which is loaded
with home-based business information ranging from "Branding
Your Business" to "In Praise of Thinking Small."

Working from Home (Paul and Sarah Edwards)

www.workingfromhome.com

> The authors of several best-selling books on self-employment, Paul and Sarah Edwards are well respected for their knowledge of and insights into working from home. Take the self-employment self-assessment quiz, read sample chapters from their books, or read through their experience-based answers to frequently asked questions. Listen to the Home-Based Business radio show (check here for the schedule), or catch archives of past shows anytime you want. You'll also find information on their fee-based services, online courses, and teleseminars.

Working Solo

www.workingsolo.com

> Working Solo extends a helping hand to the solo self-employed by providing a free monthly e-newsletter, FAQs about starting a solo business, and SOHO resources and articles. This Web site is the companion to the *Working Solo* series of books by best-selling SOHO author Terri Lonier.

Resources for Women Business Owners

SBA-Sponsored

Online Women's Business Center (OWBC)

www.onlinewbc.gov

> The U.S. has more than 10 million woman-owned businesses, and the U.S. Small Business Administration (SBA) Office of Women's Business Ownership sponsors the OWBC to help them (and newer startups) succeed. Custom view links take you to the SBA's

resources on starting, financing, and managing a business (see U.S. Small Business Administration, discussed in the first section). SBA representatives specially trained in assisting female entrepreneurs are available in every SBA regional office, and you can locate the one nearest you through this Web site. The SBA Women's Business Center Program provides a network of more than 100 educational resource centers across the country—all listed here. Learn about the Women's Network for Entrepreneurial Training (WNET) mentoring program, find answers to frequently asked questions, and get motivated by inspiring success stories. This site is also available in Spanish.

Other Resources Mainly for Women

Enterprising Women

www.enterprisingwomen.com

The companion Web site for the magazine by the same name, Enterprising Women has articles highlighting women entrepreneurs. Subscription information is available here, as are archives of past issues with plenty of interesting content. For example, past articles have included "Travel with Purpose: The Peace Corps" and "The Girls' Guide to Doing the Deal: Why Market Cycles Matter."

Internet Based Moms

www.internetbasedmoms.com

The Internet offers business opportunities your mother never had, and you can learn the ins and outs of an Internet-based business at Internet Based Moms. From advice on choosing and starting an Internet business to building an income-producing Web site to optimizing search engine results to promoting your business online, you'll find it here. Membership is free and gives you access to the busy discussion boards, the weekly e-newsletter, and the online chat rooms, as well as other resources.

Jobs and Moms Career Center

www.jobsandmoms.com

> This nicely laid-out site features many options for work-at-home moms, from starting your own business to buying a franchise, engaging in direct sales or working for an employer. In addition to specific opportunities, site author Nancy Collamer lists additional resources such as government agencies, books, and professional associations. The full-feature job board can help you locate employers who are actively recruiting work-at-home professionals.

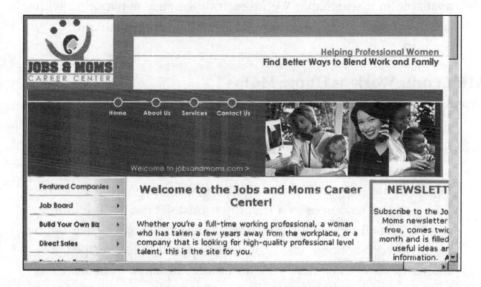

National Association for Female Executives (NAFE)

www.nafe.com

> Over 60,000 strong, NAFE is the largest women's association for professionals and business owners in the U.S. NAFE supports its members with networking opportunities, education, and public advocacy. In addition, member benefits include discounts on many personal and business services such as insurance, banking, technology, and more.

National Association of Women Business Owners (NAWBO)

www.nawbo.org

Although most of the content at this Web site is accessible only to members, you can register for a free 30-day trial membership to help evaluate its potential value to you. Like the business associations discussed earlier in this chapter, NAWBO provides member benefits such as corporate and insurance discounts and other services through a business resource center. Members' profiles are available in a searchable Web directory for easy networking with other women business owners. This site is also available in Spanish.

WAHM.com: Work at Home Moms

www.wahm.com

WAHM.com is an online magazine for work-at-home moms, a sector of the labor force with unique needs and concerns. Even the name sounds like a crying kid. But that may be intentional, judging from the generous humor dished up at this site, not to mention a ton of resources in a friendly format. These include a free weekly e-mail newsletter, telecommuting job listings, active online forums, work-at-home ideas, business opportunities, recipes, a directory of WAHMs near you, and more. Promote your business by adding information to the online WAHM directory, and don't forget to enjoy the weekly cartoon.

WomanOwned.com

www.womanowned.com

If you're interested in starting or growing a business, you'll find some good reading here. Articles range from brainstorming for ideas to recruiting and developing an advisory board. Through the membership-based business portal, you can find and network with other woman-owned businesses and continue your networking efforts in online forums, as well as access other services and benefits.

Temporary Work, Contract Employment, Freelancing, Teleworking, and Volunteering

You have more possibilities than ever these days when it comes to working. The value and benefit of temporary jobs, freelance work, contract work, and telecommuting are getting more recognition as these alternatives to 9-to-5 work are becoming less unusual and more common.

Employers can pay more for contracted or temporary work to meet specific needs or peak business activities and still save on employment costs in the long run. Individuals can use temporary or contract work to transition between jobs, gain job experience, break into a new field, avoid boredom, control their work schedules, and (often) make more money.

Then there's working for no money. The U.S. has a strong tradition of volunteer work, from the grassroots level up to nationwide. Volunteer work can pay rewards that can't be measured in dollars and cents. Whether you take on flexible work that pays well or not at all, each can provide valuable experience and can open your eyes to new careers and possibilities.

General Information on Temporary Work, Contract Employment, and Freelancing

The line between being employed or self-employed gets blurred around temp work, contract employment, and freelancing. Temps usually work for and are paid by an agency that finds positions for them and places them in various settings. Contractors may work for such an agency, may be traditionally self-employed, or may contract with an organization that functions as their "employer" while they retain full autonomy over their work (such as PACE, described in this section). Freelancers are typically self-employed in creative professions—designers, writers, artists—although they may also choose a different business model to meet their needs.

One of these needs is employment benefits, especially health insurance. If you're considering an alternative to traditional full-time employment, be sure to figure in the cost of self-paid employment benefits. Fortunately, there are viable options for you here as well, and these sites will give you leads.

AllFreelance.com Freelance Jobs Directory

www.allfreelance.com

> Anything freelance can be found through this directory. This hefty collection of freelance-related links is organized into topics: freelance job sites, freelance articles, work-at-home job sites, telecommuting jobs, online courses, project management, weekly articles, message boards, and more. Lots of reading and resources will keep you coming back.

The Contract Employee's Handbook

www.cehandbook.com

> The Contract Employee's Handbook is a great help if you're interested in or working as a skilled temporary employee. Contract employees, sometimes referred to as leased employees, are employed by a contract employment agency and assigned to work in client companies. Learn here about the types of contract

employment agencies, the types of contractors, how to work the system to your advantage, legal matters, and more. You also can sign up for a free biweekly e-mail newsletter for professional and technical contractors.

Professional Association for Contract Employment (PACE)

www.pacepros.com

PACE offers a new business model for contract professionals, whether you work independently or for a contracting agency. Through PACE, you can retain all the independence and tax advantages of being a self-employed contract professional, but PACE is your official employer of record for tax purposes, simulating a one-person corporation. PACE can also provide "back office" services such as online timesheets, invoicing, and payroll processing with direct deposit, as well as group benefits and career-support services. PACE is not a recruiting agency, but future plans call for developing a marketing center to help contract professionals market their services directly to prospective clients. The executive director of PACE is James R. Ziegler, Ph.D., author of The Contract Employee's Handbook, just described.

Work Sources for Temporary Work, Contract Employment, and Freelancing

Explore all your alternatives at these sites, which present a variety of opportunities and employment arrangements for you to consider.

Aquent

www.aquent.com

Aquent works like an agent for creative and IT professionals, helping them find projects, temp work, and full-time employment. Fill out an online application to see whether Aquent will represent you. If you are hired through Aquent, it handles billing and the other details involved in contract work and makes other benefits available, such as health, dental, and workers compensation insurance and 401(k) plans.

Creative Freelancers

www.freelancers.com

Freelance designers, illustrators, writers, editors, photographers, Web designers, and other creative types can get Internet exposure through Creative Freelancers. Enter your free profile into the database and show up in talent searches conducted by both Creative Freelancers and outside employers. Value-added information includes a pricing guide, legal help, and links to clubs, organizations, and other resources for creative professionals.

Elance Marketplace

www.elance.com/c/cats/main/sellers.pl

Elance Marketplace, a fee-based site, connects companies that have outsourcing needs with professionals who can provide those services. Service providers have a choice of different subscriptions, ranging from a free courtesy listing to a select professional package. Choose the monthly, quarterly, or yearly option, or subscribe by category to see only listings appropriate to your industry. Extensive tips guide you through the process, and sample letters and agreements are available for free.

Kelly Services

www.kellyservices.us

Kelly Services, the oldest name in temp agencies, provides employees in a variety of fields to companies around the globe. Search for contract and regular opportunities by location, category, or keyword. Check out Kelly's salary surveys, career assessment tools, book recommendations, articles, and more.

Manpower

www.manpower.com

> One of the biggest providers of staffing services with 4,300 offices worldwide, Manpower provides a searchable database of current opportunities, a list of local offices, and information on why you might want to work for Manpower. This site is also available in French and Spanish.

Monster: Contract & Temporary

http://ct.monster.com

> The main attraction of this section of Monster is its database of searchable temporary and contract positions. You can see what's available from a number of agencies and companies rather than working with just one staffing agency. Also check out career advice and resources targeted at temporary and contract workers.

Net-Temps

www.net-temps.com

Net-Temps specializes in job postings for the staffing industry, including temporary, temporary-to-permanent, and full-time positions. You can search the job listings by location and keyword or browse by category. You can also register to post your resume online (from Microsoft Word or using the resume builder tool), use job search agents, and receive postings via e-mail. When registering or searching, specify whether you'd like just contract positions or both contract and direct-hire opportunities. You can apply online for most positions. Quick apply lets you paste your resume into a form for easy sending to employers. You can also read a number of career development articles and get advice on changing careers.

Working Today

www.workingtoday.org

Independent workers—freelancers, consultants, independent contractors, temps, part-timers, contingent employees, and the self-employed—make up about 30% of the nation's workforce. As a national nonprofit, Working Today's goal is to support America's growing independent workforce through advocacy, information, and service. Join for a modest yearly fee to receive member discounts on legal and dental services, office products, and other items useful to the independent worker. An additional one-time setup fee provides access to group health insurance. Browse through helpful resources and articles for further information on topics such as benefits issues and finances.

Teleworking/Telecommuting

The most recent statistics from the U.S. Census Bureau report that nearly 20 million Americans work at least one day a week at home, either for themselves or for an employer. Cell phones, low-priced desktop and laptop computers, fax, e-mail, PDAs, and other technology allow telecommuters to keep in constant contact from home or anywhere. Challenges exist, however, such as managing your time effectively and controlling your barking dog when you're on the phone. Telecommuting is often an arrangement you make with your employer, although some companies now recruit specifically for telecommuting jobs. In addition to this section, see the "SOHO: Small Office/Home Office" and "Resources for Women Business Owners" sections in chapter 8.

Better Business Bureau: Work-at-Home Schemes

www.bbb.org/library/workathome.asp

Get savvy about work-at-home opportunities. A lot of valid ones exist, but, unfortunately, so do work-at-home scams. Falling for one is double trouble. Not only can you lose money, time, and your reputation, but you can be held liable for perpetrating a fraud, even unintentionally. Fortunately, the Better Business Bureau provides information on how to recognize and avoid being taken by phony work-at-home schemes, including a list of the most common scams and sample job ads to avoid. The best advice? If it sounds too good to be true, it probably is.

HomeworkersNet

www.homeworkersnet.com

Sign up for the free e-mail newsletter that lists work-at-home job opportunities that aren't posted online. Then go on to explore the rest of the site, including a job listings section that pulls work-at-home opportunities from a number of job banks. Each opening is researched by HomeworkersNet to help you avoid less-than-legitimate offers. Check back often for daily featured positions. Other sections include a directory of other sites devoted to home-based employment, an employer directory, home business ideas, and articles and advice.

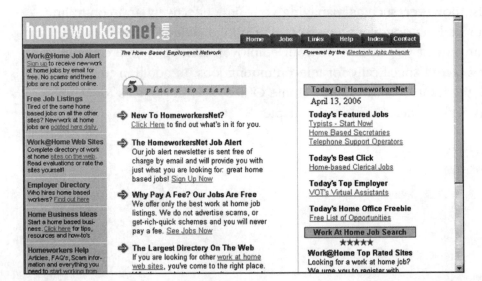

InnoVisions Canada/Canadian Telework Association

www.ivc.ca

InnoVisions Canada and the nonprofit Canadian Telework Association team up here to provide a ton of worldwide information, statistics, and resources on telecommuting. Find out about everything from telecommuting and disabilities to conferences and taxes—and everything in between.

PortaJobs

www.portajobs.com

As a job seeker, you can register for free to query the PortaJobs database for job postings, apply for openings, or store your own customized search strategies for future use. Create an online profile and sign up to receive e-mail notifications of new postings that match it. You can choose to keep your contact information confidential while having your resume and skills profile remain searchable by employers. Reports and news can help you find out more about telecommuting trends.

Telecommuting Jobs

www.tjobs.com

View free job listings in categories including artists, programmers, writers, web designers, data entry, and engineers. A low-cost membership lets you respond to job postings and post your resume online to show up in talent searches by employers. You can also create a low-cost "InSiteOffice" page that shows you mean business with a professional at-home setup. Other helpful sections include free articles and statistics, as well as links to certification, training, and other useful resources for telecommuters.

Telework Coalition

www.telcoa.org

The Telework Coalition (TelCoa) is a nonprofit organization promoting the economic, social, and environmental benefits of telecommuting. Join to get access to research reports and discounts on products and services, or just browse through the free information on this site for conference dates, articles, quick facts, and related links.

YouCanWorkFromAnywhere.com

www.youcanworkfromanywhere.com

Telecommuters, mobile workers, road warriors, and home-based workers can find tips, articles, classes, e-books, newsletters, and more on working effectively in nontraditional ways. Find out how to use technology effectively while telecommuting, such as by locating Wi-Fi (wireless technology) hotspots to get online. This comprehensive site is a great place to find information on getting started as a telecommuter and working more effectively from home.

Volunteer Opportunities

Have you looked at volunteering lately? There's executive volunteering, mid-career volunteering, volunteering vacations, volunteer matching, and virtual volunteering. Volunteering "jobs" range from one week (at Global Volunteers, described in this section) to the 27 months required by the Peace Corps (also described in this section). Volunteering can give you valuable experience for your resume and the intangible benefit of making a difference in the world.

1-800-Volunteer.org

www.1-800-volunteer.org

1-800-Volunteer.org is "America's Address for Volunteering." Here you can get connected to volunteer opportunities in your community (or elsewhere where your talents are needed), track your volunteer service, and receive automatic e-mail notifications when you're needed most. Find a volunteer opportunity by searching by issue area or zip code. If no opportunities exist in your area, no problem—the organization also lists virtual volunteer jobs that you can do from home. This site also is available in Spanish.

American Red Cross

www.redcross.org/services/volunteer/

> If you feel the urge to help out but giving blood makes you squeamish, check the American Red Cross's Web site for other volunteer opportunities. In addition to its blood bank, the American Red Cross is well-known for its disaster relief services, health and safety skills training, and more. Read all about it at this Web site, including articles and inspirational stories from volunteers. Locate your local chapter by zip code.

Citizens Development Corps

www.cdc.org

> The Citizens Development Corps is devoted to economic development in emerging and transitioning economies worldwide through the use of experienced business professionals. A network of more than 7,000 expert volunteer advisors from every industry and skill set provides programs dealing with association building, export promotion, job creation, policy and regulatory reform, privatization, procurement and supplier training, and more. Learn about the benefits of volunteering and the participation requirements, and browse the currently open assignments.

Corporation for National & Community Service

www.cns.gov

This federally funded site offers three major opportunities for public service. Through AmeriCorps, volunteers devote a year to giving back to the community through educational, environmental, health, and public safety services. Senior Corps taps the skills of older citizens through foster grandparents, senior companions, and other volunteer opportunities. Learn and Serve America lets the younger generation combine volunteerism with education through their schools. Find out about these programs, search for other volunteer opportunities, or connect with other members or service alums.

Global Volunteers

www.globalvolunteers.org

Take a different kind of vacation by volunteering abroad or in the U.S. in community development projects that last one to three weeks. Service projects with Global Volunteers range from tutoring and teaching English to childcare, construction, and healthcare. No specialized skills are required. Find out whether the program is right for you by reading the FAQs, checking out different service programs, or subscribing to the e-newsletter.

Idealist

www.idealist.org

Idealist brings together nonprofit organizations, nonprofit professionals, and volunteers with a searchable database of opportunities. Sign up to have new work or volunteer opportunities e-mailed to you and to have your skills listed in the database so that organizations can easily find you. Other neat ideas here include volunteering with your family, volunteering abroad, and making a career out of nonprofit work by searching Idealist's career center for jobs and internships with these organizations. You can also search for or browse organizations by area of interest or geographic location to find out who is doing what and participate in online discussion groups. This site also is available in Spanish and French.

International Executive Service Corps (IESC)

www.iesc.org

IESC is a professional economic development organization that uses volunteer experts, professional staff, and strategic partners. It provides a wide range of services, such as technical, managerial, and professional consulting; trade and investment services; small grants administration; training programs; international standards certification; and more. Funded primarily through the U.S. Agency for International Development, IESC operates in more than 60 countries. Read the FAQs, or, better yet, read the firsthand accounts of IESC volunteers, and then register online if you meet the qualifications.

Peace Corps

www.peacecorps.gov

Find out about recruiting events, e-mail or find a recruiter, or apply online to serve overseas as a Peace Corps volunteer. The Peace Corps needs volunteers in areas such as education, information technology, agriculture, health, environment, business, and community development. Read through stories from volunteers to find out what volunteering abroad is really like, read news stories, and find out about other benefits such as student loan deferment, job placement, and training services for returned volunteers. This site also is available in French and Spanish.

Points of Light Foundation

www.pointsoflight.org

The Points of Light Foundation was organized in 1990 for the purpose of engaging more people more effectively in volunteer community service to help solve serious social problems. Here you can locate your local Points of Light volunteer center, find out about the foundation mission and programs, and access other resources. The Points of Light Foundation and the Volunteer Center National Network Council collaboratively sponsor 1-800-Volunteer.org (described earlier in this section).

SERVEnet

www.servenet.org

SERVEnet is a free matching service for volunteers and organizations. Either do a quick search by zip code to list organizations and opportunities in your area, or use the advanced search to more closely match your skills to available opportunities. You can find out about special volunteer events across the nation, virtual (online) volunteer opportunities, and how to be a successful volunteer. If you register and create a profile, local nonprofits can notify you about volunteer opportunities that match your skills, interests, and schedule. SERVEnet is a program of Youth Service America.

Teach For America

www.teachforamerica.org

New and recent college graduates with a desire to teach and a sense of adventure will want to check out this Web site. Teach For America is a public service program that places trained corps members in schools that have a critical need for qualified, certified teachers. The program accepts students from many academic disciplines, not just education. Successful program applicants complete an intensive five-week residential summer institute before getting their two-year assignments. Subscribe to the free applicant newsletter, fill out an online application, and find out more about the program at this Web site.

United Nations Volunteers

www.unv.org

Each year, nearly 5,000 volunteers from more than 150 countries contribute their efforts to the United Nations Volunteers program, which works through United Nations Development Programme offices around the world. Learn about the recruitment process for volunteering abroad, and find out how to apply to volunteer at home, abroad, or even online. For inspiration, read about the experiences of UN volunteers working for peace and development around the globe.

VolunteerMatch

www.volunteermatch.org

> As the name suggests, VolunteerMatch provides a free matching service for volunteers and organizations. Put in your zip code to find places to volunteer in your area, or choose the virtual volunteering option and browse through ways to contribute your skills without leaving home. This Web site also lets you create a personal volunteer account to receive personalized e-mails and manage your online volunteer resume. Get inspired reading the volunteer stories showcased each month.

Volunteer-Related Associations

If you're interested in a career either with a nonprofit or in the field of volunteerism, these associations may give you some ideas to pursue.

Alliance for Nonprofit Management

www.allianceonline.org

> The Alliance for Nonprofit Management is devoted to the management and government of nonprofit organizations. Its Resource Center is an annotated, searchable database of organizations, Web sites, books, newsletters, and other products and services for nonprofit organizations. This Web site also includes an online CareerBank, which can be searched by location and position type, as well as a free online newsletter.

Association of Fundraising Professionals

www.nsfre.org

> Fund-raising requires a special set of skills. If you have these skills and you want to put them to good use in a career helping a nonprofit raise badly needed funds, this is the organization for you. This Web site provides information on how the association promotes charitable giving. It also shows you how you can develop your career and education as a fundraising professional.

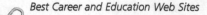

National Council of Nonprofit Associations (NCNA)

www.ncna.org

> NCNA is a network of state and regional nonprofit associations representing over 22,000 members in 46 states and the District of Columbia. Its mission includes raising the profile of nonprofits and providing them with the tools and leadership they need to function more effectively. Find out about current projects, locate your state association, browse job openings with member associations and partners, and find out about events in your area.

Today's Volunteer

www.asdvs.org

> Hospitals are a major "employer" of volunteers, and the American Society of Directors of Volunteer Services is the only national professional organization for directors of volunteer services in healthcare. At their Web site, Today's Volunteer, you can learn about ways to manage healthcare volunteers effectively, read up on news and events, find out about conferences and educational opportunities, and search for volunteer opportunities.

Glossary

ACT (American College Testing Assessment)   A standardized college admissions test measuring a student's scholastic development. Most colleges base admissions decisions on a combination of grades, activities, and scores on standardized tests such as this or the SAT.

address book   In your e-mail client software, the list of names and addresses of people to whom you frequently send messages.

affiliate program   An agreement between Web-based businesses to direct viewers to other Web sites through links, usually with a commission for resulting sales.

apprenticeship   A job-training program that combines classroom lessons with on-the-job training.

autoresponder   An e-mail software feature that automatically sends a response to each incoming e-mail message. For example, if a Web site instructs you to subscribe to its newsletter by sending an e-mail with "subscribe" in the subject line and you receive an immediate response, the site is using an autoresponder to manage newsletter subscriptions.

blog   Short for Web log. A Web site that serves as a publicly available personal journal.

BLS (U.S. Department of Labor Bureau of Labor Statistics)   The primary federal source of data on employment.

bookmarks   In Netscape Navigator, a way to save the addresses of your favorite Web sites so that you can return to them easily in the future. This feature is called "Favorites" in Microsoft Internet Explorer.

Boolean logic   The form of logic used by many search engines that allows you to control how narrow or broad a search you want to conduct by combining search terms in certain ways. Named for mathematician George Boole.

bot Short for "robot." A software tool sent out by a search engine to dig through the Web for your requested information.

broadband access A high-speed way to connect to the Internet using cable television networks or upgraded phone lines that use technologies such as Integrated Services Digital Network (ISDN) and Digital Subscriber Line (DSL). See also *dial-up access*.

browser A program used to view Web pages. The most well-known browser programs are Microsoft Internet Explorer and Netscape Navigator. You also might encounter other browsers, such as Mozilla and Opera.

bulletin board See *forum*.

career information Descriptions of careers that might include attributes such as job requirements, skills, educational preparation, working conditions, employment outlook, and wages.

chat To communicate online in real time. The person with whom you are chatting can see your words as you type them or immediately after you press Enter. Also called *instant messaging* or *IM*.

clearinghouse A Web site that contains lists of other Web sites, organized by related topics.

continuing education 1. Courses available to adults who are not enrolled in a formal degree program. 2. Education undertaken after you complete a degree program to remain current in your field, sometimes required for maintaining licensure or certification. Continuing-education credits may be awarded for courses, workshops, or conferences.

contracting Providing specific services to a company for a specified period of time and for a specified payment.

cookie A text-only string that gets entered into a browser's memory. It allows Web sites to personalize information, help with online sales or service, or collect demographic information.

cover letter A letter written to accompany a resume. It expresses your interest in the position you are applying for and gives an overview of your skills.

database An organized collection of data that you can access and sort by selected criteria. For example, a job bank is an online database of available jobs. You could direct it to sort only the jobs in your state, as opposed to those across the country.

demographics   Data about the age, race, sex, income, and other details of people living in a certain area. Applications of demographic data include targeting advertising or getting an idea of the labor market in a particular area.

dial-up access   A way to connect to the Internet over standard telephone lines. Dial-up used to be found in the majority of homes, but this is no longer true. About half of all homes have dial-up. The rest use faster broadband connections. See also *broadband access*.

Dictionary of Occupational Titles (DOT)   A reference publication, based on U.S. Department of Labor data, that classifies and briefly describes more than 12,000 jobs.

directory   A place on a computer or server where data files are stored. Directories are used to separate files into related groups and specify the location of the files on the computer.

discussion board   A Web site function that allows users to post questions or comments and respond to other people's postings. Discussion boards are commonly organized by topics or "threads."

distance learning   The ability to further your education, either toward a degree or as part of your lifelong learning, by taking courses through learning technologies other than a traditional classroom. These technologies include audiotapes, videotapes, teleconferencing, videoconferencing, and computer-based and Internet-based training.

DOL (U.S. Department of Labor)   The federal agency that oversees all federally funded labor-related programs.

domain   1. The part of your e-mail address that specifies the name of the ISP through which you access your e-mail, such as aol.com. 2. The part of a Web address that identifies the presence of a company or organization on the Internet.

download   To copy files from the Internet to your computer's hard drive.

e-lancer   A self-employed individual who contracts for work primarily through the Internet.

electronic resume   Any resume in a computerized format, usually in Microsoft Word, ASCII text, HTML, or PDF.

e-mail   Electronic mail. A written message sent from one person's online address to another's via the Internet or another computer network.

e-mail discussion list An e-mail group in which a message posted by any member is disseminated to all members of the group, any of whom are free to respond and participate in the discussion.

emoticon A sideways symbol in e-mail that is composed of keyboard characters. It indicates the mood of the person writing the message. For example, :) is a smiley face.

ETA (U.S. Department of Labor Employment and Training Administration) The federal agency responsible for federally funded employment and training programs.

FAQs (Frequently Asked Questions) A list of answers to the questions that Web site visitors are likely to ask repeatedly.

Favorites In Internet Explorer, a way to save the addresses of your favorite Web sites so that you can return to them easily in the future. This feature is called "bookmarks" in Netscape Navigator.

file name The name of the document that contains the data on a Web page. Many Web page file names end with the letters .htm or .html.

financial aid The combination of scholarships, grants, and loans that a student uses to pay for college. Financial aid is limited to the amount of "need" that is determined for the student.

flex work Nontraditional work arrangements such as contracting, freelancing, and temporary work.

forum An online discussion group. Sometimes called a *bulletin board*.

franchise A business in which you buy the right to use the name and the established procedures and products in exchange for a percentage of the profits.

free agent A self-employed individual who works on a contract basis, often for more than one employer.

freelancer A self-employed individual who works on a contract basis, often for more than one employer.

freeware Software (such as games and utilities) that you can download from the Internet and use for free.

FTP (File Transfer Protocol) A protocol for transferring files from one computer to another over the Internet.

graphical user interface (GUI) The graphical menus, tools, and buttons you see on-screen, which help you work with a particular program using the mouse's point-and-click features.

GRE (Graduate Record Exam)   The test taken by college seniors for admission to graduate programs.

guaranty agency   The state agency or private, nonprofit organization that administers federally funded student loans.

home page   1. A Web site's initial page or starting page. 2. The page you set to appear when you first open your browser or click the Home button.

host   Any computer on a network that is a repository for services available to other computers on the network.

HTML (Hypertext Markup Language)   The coding that is used to turn regular text into a Web page that can be viewed by a browser.

hyperlink (link)   A word, phrase, or graphic on a Web page that is connected to another Internet document. By clicking it, you are taken to a related Web page, either on the same site or on a completely different Web site.

hypertext   Text that contains one or more hyperlinks.

independent professional   A self-employed individual who works on a contract basis, often for more than one employer.

indexed search engine   A search engine, such as AltaVista, that locates Web pages based on text found on the page or keywords in metatags hidden in a document's coding.

infrastructure   The essential, underlying elements of an entity or organization that allow it to function.

instant messaging   See *chat*.

Internet directory   Reviews and organizes the information on the Web into categories. Each broad category, such as "Business & Economy," has more specific categories under it, and those categories have even more specific categories under them. Yahoo! is an example of an Internet directory.

Internet Explorer   Microsoft's Internet browser program, used to view and move between Web pages. Internet Explorer is built into Microsoft Windows.

Internet Service Provider (ISP)   A national or local company that, for a monthly fee, lets you connect to the Internet. Examples of national ISPs include America Online, AT&T WorldNet, and Earthlink.

internship   A program in which a student works for an employer for a specified period of time to learn about a particular occupation. The intern is sometimes paid for the work in addition to receiving college credit.

interview To meet with a potential employer that has a job opening to determine whether you are the right person for the job. In an informational interview, you meet with a person who works in the field in which you are interested so that you can learn about the job and what you need to do to prepare for it.

job bank A Web database of job openings. You can search for specific jobs by title, category, and geographic location, among other variables.

Job Corps A federally funded residential education and job-training program for at-risk youth ages 16 to 24.

job fair A meeting at which employers set up booths and speak with job seekers in an effort to recruit employees.

keyword 1. A word you type into a search engine or Web site search function to help locate information you are seeking. 2. A "hot" word (usually a noun) used in a resume. It is associated with a specific industry, profession, or job function.

labor market The pool of both employed and unemployed persons who are currently available and willing to work; the source of applicants for a job opening.

labor market information Data about workers, jobs, industries, and employers, generally used by program planners, analysts, administrators, researchers, employers, and job seekers.

leased employee Someone who works for a company that sells his or her services to another company for a specified period of time. The leasing company (or temporary agency) administers the employee's salaries and benefits. See also *temp*.

link (hyperlink) A word, phrase, or graphic on a Web page that is connected to another Internet document. By clicking it, you are taken to a related Web page, either on the same site or on a completely different Web site.

listserv™ Trademarked e-mail discussion-management software from the L-soft Corporation, often misused as a generic term for an e-mail discussion list.

load To open a Web page with your browser. The computer temporarily copies the data from the server onto your computer's hard drive.

Macintosh (Mac)   A computer introduced by Apple Computer in 1984. The Macintosh was distinguished by its graphical user interface, which allowed users to point and click with a mouse in addition to using a keyboard to operate the system.

mailing list   A list of e-mail addresses to which you can send the same e-mail message simultaneously.

message board   A place on a Web site where people can post and respond to questions and discussion topics. See also *forum*.

metalist   A list of related Web sites posted on a Web site. Also known as a *clearinghouse*.

metasearch engine   A search engine that lets you use several search engines at a time after entering your search criteria only once.

Microsoft   The software company that introduced the Internet Explorer browser program and the Windows operating system, among other programs.

modem   The device (either inside or outside your computer) that translates information from your computer and from remote resources into a format that can travel over telephone lines.

multithreaded search engine   See *metasearch engine*.

Netscape   The software company that produced the Netscape Navigator browser program for viewing Web pages.

network   Two or more computers or other devices connected to one another and capable of sharing data. The Internet is a massive, worldwide computer network.

networking   Using your personal contacts to learn about careers and possible job openings.

newsgroup   A topical online discussion group in which you can read and post messages. You can access newsgroups over the Web at http://groups.google.com.

occupational information   Employment data such as wages, anticipated growth, number of people employed, number of new jobs, and other trends.

Occupational Outlook Handbook (OOH)   A reference publication based on U.S. Department of Labor data. It describes the 250 most popular jobs, covering approximately 85 percent of the workforce.

O*NET   The U.S. Department of Labor's electronic database of career and job information on specific occupations.

on-the-job training   Job training that occurs in the workplace.

path   The location of a Web page on a server. It includes the domain name, directories, and file name.

PDA (personal digital assistant)   Usually includes scheduler, address book, task list, clock, and calculator software. A PDA can be synched with a desktop computer, and many can now access the Internet through Wi-Fi or other technology.

phishing   An Internet scam that attempts to collect private user information to be used for identity theft. You receive an e-mail directing you to an authentic-looking Web site, where you are asked to update personal information, such as passwords and credit card, Social Security, and bank account numbers. A legitimate Web site or organization would already have these. To protect yourself from phishing, never provide personal information to a Web site based on an e-mail request.

PIN (personal identification number)   A number you select or that is assigned to you for the purpose of verifying your identification for Internet transactions.

plugin   A software program that works with your browser to display added information. Examples of plugins include Adobe Acrobat Reader and Macromedia Flash.

Portable Document Format (PDF or .pdf)   A file format that allows documents created in any software program and saved in this format to be read through the freely downloadable Adobe Acrobat Reader software. Allows documents to appear and be printed exactly as their creator intended.

protocol   An agreed-upon format for transferring data from one computer to another.

query   To ask a database to sort and show you all the data that meets your specified criteria.

Really Simple Syndication (RSS)   A format that Web sites use to send updated headlines around the Internet. RSS allows for the automatic distribution of Internet content from news-related sites via RSS aggregators or readers, letting you receive free updates by subscribing (or clicking buttons labeled RSS or XML) to information from sites that publish content, such as news outlets or bloggers. You need an RSS reader to read a news feed.

Reserves   Military personnel who are not on active duty but who can be called into duty during a war or national crisis.

resume   An organized, written summary of your work experience, education, skills, and qualifications. Many job postings request that you submit a resume for consideration.

resume bank   A Web site where you can post a copy of your resume for potential employers to view.

robot (bot)   A software tool sent out by a search engine to dig through the Web for your requested information.

ROTC (Reserve Officer Training Corps)   A cooperative program between colleges and branches of the military that allows undergraduates to receive officer training while they attend college.

SAT (Scholastic Aptitude Test)   A standardized college admissions test. Most colleges base admissions decisions on a combination of grades, activities, and scores on standardized tests such as this or the ACT.

search engine   A Web site that lets you search for other Web sites of interest by entering a keyword or keywords in a search field. Examples of search engines include Google and AltaVista.

self-assessment   The process of working to identify, understand, and express your skills, knowledge, abilities, interests, values, personality, motivations, passions, and anything else about you that might affect your career decisions.

server   A computer, connected to a network, that manages resources such as files or printers. Web servers contain and serve up Web page documents in response to requests from browsers.

service academy   An undergraduate college run by a branch of the armed forces that trains high school graduates to be military officers.

shareware   Software that you can download from the Internet and use for a small fee.

signature   Information that automatically appears at the bottom of every e-mail you send. It can include your name, your contact information, or your favorite quote. You can change your signature to say whatever you want.

Small Business Administration (SBA)   The federal government's primary source of small-business assistance programs under the U.S. Department of Commerce.

software   A computer program that performs a specific task. Examples of software include Internet browsers, word-processing programs, spreadsheets, and games.

SOHO (small office/home office)   An acronym that reflects the growing trend of self-employed people operating small businesses from inside or outside their home environment.

teleworker (telecommuter, home worker)   An employee who works at least part-time in a home office, communicating with coworkers and clients via telephone, fax, instant messaging, and/or e-mail.

temp   A person who is employed by an agency to fill short-term positions in other companies. This person's salary and benefits are paid by the agency rather than by the companies.

TOEFL (Test of English as a Foreign Language)   Used to determine whether students are ready for mainstream classes with native speakers of English.

traffic (site traffic)   The volume of users who view a particular Web site. Increased traffic helps the owner sell advertising on the site.

upload   To send files from your computer to an Internet location.

URL (Uniform Resource Locator)   A Web site's address, such as http://www.jist.com. The first part (http://) specifies the protocol for the computers to use when transferring data; the second part specifies the computer and domain name of the site you are accessing.

user name   Your unique identifier on a computer system. Many Web sites that ask you to register require you to select a user name. You use this user name and a private password to gain access again later.

Web page   A document located on another computer elsewhere on the Internet that you can view with a browser; one page within a Web site.

Web site   A group of related Web pages, compiled and sponsored by an individual or organization.

Welfare to Work   Federal welfare reform legislation intended to transition welfare recipients to the paid workforce.

Wi-Fi   Short for wireless technology network. Wi-Fi allows laptops and PDAs to connect to the Internet at high speeds without the use of wires.

Windows   Microsoft's graphical user interface and operating system for IBM-compatible PCs.

workforce   The sector of the population that is currently employed or that is ready, willing, and able to work.

workforce development   Initiatives and programs addressing the growth and maintenance of an educated, skilled workforce, coordinating with multiple employment and training service providers.

Workforce Investment Act (WIA) of 1998   Federal legislation that replaced the federal Job Training Partnership Act in 2000.

Workforce Investment Board   A policy-setting board that administers programs under the federal Workforce Investment Act, which took effect in 2000.

World Wide Web (WWW or "the Web")   A global network of information that is based on hyperlinks, which let the viewer easily jump from one Web page or Web site to a related page or site.

Index